The Streets & the Stars

Clwyd Poetry Project

Bits and Pieces

We must glean the fields in the world as it is, for bits and pieces gather everywhere, tinder of the wind and the rain in the river mouth, worthless little twigs on the lawn, fragments of cobweb in the wasting away of autumn, heaps of leaves at the bottoms of ditches, old circulars, committee reports, clichés of devotion and creed in the mind's attic, dust, debris and ashbins, overspill of peevish smoke on chimneys, and rusty old tins in the river bed.

Why talk of stray bits and pieces like these, and bother to note them? — odds-and-ends of observation that matter to no one and nothing...

A man came by with a lorry today, collecting old iron to be cast into Brymbo's furnaces...

Why talk of bits and pieces?
— Because the scrap melts to a message in the poem.

Euros Bowen
(translated from the Welsh by Joseph Clancy)

The Streets & the Stars

An anthology of writing from Wales
edited by John Davies and Melvyn Jones

SEREN BOOKS

SEREN BOOKS is the book imprint of
Poetry Wales Press Ltd.
Andmar House, Tondu Road,
Bridgend, Mid-Glamorgan

British Library Cataloguing in Publication Data:

The Streets and the Stars: Anthology of Writing from Wales
I. Davies, John
II. Jones, Melvyn
820.8

ISBN: 1-85411-076-4

Cover artwork: Looking Out, 1986, by Ernest Zobole.

The publisher acknowledges the financial support of the Welsh Arts Council

Typeset in 11 point New Century Schoolbook by Megaron, Cardiff
Printed by The Cromwell Press,
Broughton Gifford, Melksham,
Wiltshire SN12 8PH

Contents

Creatures

Dialogues

Portraits

The Earth

Foreword

Wales in English

Chatting with the caretaker of a country chapel and agreeing that it was a fine building, the poet Waldo Williams remarked that it was rather small though. 'Yes,' replied the caretaker, 'but it's big inside!' The poet remembered this when he came to write (in Welsh) the poem 'What is Man?' It begins: 'What is it to be alive?' and Waldo Williams' answer is 'To have a wide hall between narrow walls'. So with Wales whose population is one per cent of the European Community's. In its literatures' wide hall, that in Welsh began in the sixth century while that written in English, Anglo-Welsh literature, is four hundred years old. The dragon's two tongues have spoken long and eloquently, albeit to a minority in our schools.

This English coursebook for fourteen to sixteen year-olds draws its source material from both literatures and also includes responses to Wales by some English-born writers. Its publication embodies the belief that pupils should have access to poetry and prose reflecting the country in which they live, a belief explored at some length in the Welsh Office Report, *The Literature of Wales in the Secondary School* (1987). To look out at the world beyond oneself is essential; equally so to know where one is looking from. Literature being a mirror in which we see ourselves, many teachers have come to see value in introducing to pupils at least some literature reflecting their own cultural and social landscapes. Literature does not come only from the land of Elsewhere. Affirming the value of a child's own place in the world involves sharpening his or her perception of it.

Such an emphasis will, it is hoped, stimulate pupils' writing and talk as well as their wider reading, and enrich their sense of being alive in Wales. And what is that like? asks Waldo Williams. 'Keeping house among a cloud of witnesses.'

To the Teacher

Chosen for their vividness and accessibility, the selections here include short stories, poetry, reportage, and extracts from radio plays. The book emphasises equally subject matter and technique. It begins with the individual and his/her sense of place. Then it focusses on personal relationships, widening to include the animal world and the environment. Linked with particular teaching aims, these themes give rise to written English and Literature GCSE coursework, also to oral work.

Four of the seven themes are approached in the same way:

A) **Words in Focus** concentrates on individual pieces of writing. The notes here are partly informational, partly interrogative, to introduce the teaching aim.

B) **Voices** is a compilation illustrating the theme and aim, including, too, matters for discussion.

C) Then **Suggestions** offers stimuli to oral summings-up and assignments for English and Literature coursework.

The other three themes are approached through a poetry workshop, through short radio plays and reportage. It is a structure which offers a framework while leaving the teacher room for manoeuvre as regards, for example, which responses should be oral and which written.

John Davies and Melvyn Jones

Many thanks to those teachers who read patiently and commented usefully on sections of the manuscript: Beth Archard, Cynffig Comprehensive, Kenfig Hill; Cary Archard, Brynteg Comprehensive, Bridgend; Christine Evans, Ysgol Glan y Môr, Pwllheli; Dewi Evans, Ysgol Glan Clwyd, St. Asaph; Jill Fisher, Ysgol Bryn Elian, Colwyn Bay; Mike Jenkins, Pen-y-Dre High, Merthyr Tydfil; Julia Mainardis, Prestatyn High; John Metcalfe, The Groves School, Wrexham; Andrew Thomas, Y Pant Comprehensive, Talbot Green.

***

THEME	MAIN TEACHING AIM	GENRE	ASSIGNMENTS
1. Myself	Writing interestingly	Autobiographical prose (and 2 poems)	(a) Oral (b) Eng. coursework
2. Places	Writng vividly	Poetry (and 2 prose pieces)	(a) Oral (b) Eng. & Literature coursework
3. Relationships	Making judgements	3 short stories	(a) Oral (b) Eng. & Literature coursework
4. Creatures	The sounds words make	Poetry (and 2 prose pieces)	(a) Oral (b) Eng. & Literature coursework
5. Dialogue	Writing a radio play	Extracts from 3 radio plays	(a) Oral (b) Eng. coursework
6. Portraits	A Poetry Workshop	Poetry	(a) Eng. coursework
7. The Earth	Reporting	Green journalism	(a) Oral (b) Eng. coursework

Myself

Words in Focus

This first section of the book is about ourselves. Especially it's about growing up, our self-discoveries. To remember and think about them is to be more richly ourselves. We weren't born this way. What has helped make us? Writing about what has happened to us, writing autobiography, is like fishing fragments of ourselves from the everyday flow, a kind of rescue.

I

I is the biggest word
in the English language —
some people yawn bored
as soon as you mention it.

I know people who erect crosses
made from it
and then refuse to carry them.

I know people who build extensions
onto it and call
those extensions their children.

I know people who would
like to keep changing it
every week like fashionable clothing.

I know people who hate it so much
it's become an obsession,
like a priest always ranting against sin.

In English, 'I' begins the sentence:
the other words queue up behind it
waiting for their instructions.

You must write 'I' with a capital letter
but 'we' with a small one.
Why?... Well... as in God and Great Britain.

i know a person who tries to make it
mock itself, to disguise an ambition.
i know a person who thinks it will outlive
the exploring body, the inflated mind.

Mike Jenkins

Discussion

The poem lists some of the attitudes people have towards themselves. Which did you find the clearest or most recognisable? Is it possible to 'keep changing' oneself, as the poet suggests?

*

Word pictures that make comparisons are often more interesting than plain statements. Referring to people 'who erect crosses' over their lives, for instance, is a sharper way of saying something like, 'I know people full of self-pity who see their lives as endless misery'. What is suggested to you by other images in the poem: *extensions, fashionable clothing, queue* ?

*

Why did Mike Jenkins decide to begin nearly every stanza in the same way, until the ending?

*

In what way might 'we' , near the end, be more important than 'I'?

Writing Interestingly

In the following pages, writers relive episodes in their lives, making sense of memories vital to them. And the way they say it is as important as what they say. How could they hope to be read if they didn't write interestingly? As Mike Jenkins notes in his poem, 'some people yawn bored' when they hear others start to talk about themselves.

George

Brought up in Glanrafon, a village near Holywell in northeast Wales, the writer and actor Emlyn Williams describes a dramatic interruption one afternoon at his primary school. (A termagant is a violent woman.)

Mischief was one thing, evil another. One warm mid-day a week later, it was arithmetic again: the squeak of chalk on the board, the room sleepily and ominously still. Seven eights fifty-six, eight eights... The door opened like a whirlwind, somebody strode in, up to Miss Dawson, and in the tolerant sunlight that blinks at nothing, struck her across the face.

Her sudden whimper, like a dog run over, would have been enough of a shock; but coming from one who a second before had been the all-powerful adult ('Hywel Davies, mark my words, you will get the cane!') it was shattering. The attacker was, unbelievably, a woman, a termagant with a lantern-jaw and a man's cap. In the sickened silence, Miss Dawson, suddenly a white and terrified girl, uttered one English word, which I have never heard spoken since. 'Blaggard,' she gasped, rhyming it with laggard, 'blaggard!' — years later I realized that the word is written 'blackguard'. 'Dyna wers iti,' said the intruder, 'that'll teach thee, teacher!' and strode out. Miss Dawson looked at us, bewildered, burst into tears and scurried. We sat dumbfounded; I felt a wave of shame that it should be a creature of Welsh tongue and blood that had committed such an outrage, and with it a disgust, rooted in some loam of chivalry, that a woman should so demean both herself and another. Her child had apparently been detained; she was from Tai Trap, Trap's Houses, a row of slums near Rhewl Fawr. A master hurried in and took flustered charge.

But full in the face of childhood, cruelty had defeated authority; into the Headmaster's bland smile I spelt fear, and saw him crumple into a corner, an overturned scarecrow with a slate broken over his pate. We had felt earthquake, and could never be quite so footsure again.

***

Discussion

Remembering a moment when his way of looking at the world was changed suddenly, Emlyn Williams describes not just the event but the working of his mind. He aims to sweep us into his life. He wants us to believe in it, share it. So he includes details that convince us, sounds (squeak, whimper, gasped) as well as things seen: a warm drowsy room, a blackboard, numbers. Which details capture Miss Dawson's sense of shock?

*

There are other images that are comparisons. We see the door open 'like a whirlwind', the woman teacher as 'a white and terrified girl'. Why write 'Into the Headmaster's bland smile I *spelt* fear' rather than, 'saw fear'? And what is suggested by the very last sentence?

*

Notice too that the relaxed calm of the classroom is presented in drowsily short sentences. It's a warm day. Another boring lesson...Then the door bangs and the explosive arrival of the big-jawed woman is captured partly by the surging movement of the sentence, its rhythm. As well as writing *about* things, we can make them run, stumble, walk, to make our meaning more vivid.

*

Try turning these four short sentences into one flowing sentence. Rearrange words, get rid of unimportant ones if you like — but keep the essential meaning and don't use 'and' more than once:

> I ran from the room. I was shaking. The woman had struck me in front of my own class. I felt I could never return.

Autobiography

A novelist and writer of short stories, Margiad Evans lived from the age of eleven in the Border country, first at Ross-on-Wye.

November. I am twelve years old, reading on the window sill in the fruit shed. I am kneeling on a wicker hamper, and my knees are numb. The daylight is cold and cramped. Rubbing my hands I sniff the air. The hamper is full of old newspapers and the atmosphere tastes of them and of pearskins and mouldy portmanteaux.

I have read myself out of existence. No such person inhabits the dark day; but suddenly I come awake with a rush of feeling. My crowded head feels suddenly clear, empty and airy as craning out of the window, I look hungrily around. This is real, I think, the colours, the brick, the ivy. It is as though something is going to be shown to me, once and forever. Things seem so *clear;* they seem to declare themselves aloud. My eyes have touch, my skin on which the air plays seems to be as glass through which I can look from every pore. Awake, awake to all, I know it is a rare moment, perhaps a beginning of a life separate from ordinary existence.

And yet what is there? The elm tree dropping leaves yellow golden all over, into the rainwater tank. They slide slowly downward on the point and settle with the faintest breath of sound on the olive surface. And below them, in the cube of water, like things tranced in ice are others suspended on edge and rotting. Then there is the pipe, and the grey cobwebs stretched across the corners of the tank, and then suddenly the bright shadow of the tree itself with all its stars of sky — lovely but gone almost before it can be lovely.

I lean out, sighing with the strange feeling in me. I can touch the cold sides of the tank; I feel as though I can touch with my mind the tree trunk, the hedge, the hurdle, even the farthest hill that I can see. What are all these familiar things saying so clearly? Why have I never seen them like this before? A moment ago they existed but quietly and without me. Now the leaves keep falling so queerly — queerly as though I had something to do with their falling. Something is happening which makes me able to say and know that it is true: 'I shall remember this. I shall remember each vein on each leaf. I shall be able to see this whenever I want to, wherever I am!'

***

Discussion

It's mainly through our senses that we know we're alive. Emlyn Williams remembered his mind in action but in Margiad Evans' moment of self-discovery all her senses are alert to swarming details, including sight ('the colours, the bricks, the ivy...') and smell ('I sniff the air'). Where in the passage are her senses of taste and hearing triggered?

*

Images often make connections between two things. What do these images suggest to you?

> 'The bright shadow of the tree itself with all its stars of sky'
>
> 'My eyes have touch'
>
> 'I have read myself out of existence'

*

Depending on their meaning, short sentences can suggest sleepiness or... What mood do the short sentences in the second paragraph suggest to you?

*

Having read the third paragraph again, try to decide why the writer chose to make that last sentence the longest, most flowing one.

*

Since this is a past experience, why did Margiad Evans decide to write in the present tense?

*

'What are all these familiar things saying so clearly? Why have I never seen them like this before?' Keep yourself in mind as you read the autobiographical passages that follow. Everything in your life, including yesterday, is your material. But what to select? What in your life makes you say 'I shall remember this'?

Voices

Print of a Hare's Foot

Born in Clydach Vale in the Rhondda Valley, Rhys Davies lived almost entirely (except for a period during the Second World War) by the writing of novels and short stories. In his autobiography, he recounts an early romance.

I married when I was twelve. The union was brief, its ceremony and crowning act enacted in a coke oven, and the parting of husband and wife immediate.

The disused coke ovens, used in bygone days for carbonization of inferior coal, had belonged to a small, pioneering mine sloping down into the mountain-side across the bridged river. Ten of them, they ranged along a grassy bank, iron doors still hanging loose on several of the beehive-like structures. Old strips of corrugated zinc covered the holes in the arched brick roofs of those which were used now for keeping pigs and chickens in. A billy goat lived in one. In the one next to it card-playing gamblers foregathered on their atheistic Sundays; they kept wooden boxes there for seats and a table, and the rusty door hid the sinners from sight. I married Vanna in this one.

She was a dark girl of exotic Italy, with a mushroom-pale skin, her face eager as the black mane of strong curls running down to her shoulders. Born among us, like her brother Aldo, her parents had come childless from North Italy to Clydach Vale in its genesis days. Young colliers congregated in their pop, ice-cream and sweets shop, which had benches and penny-in-the-slot machines. Aldo, with whom I was friendly, sometimes gave me a free ice-cream cornet from the painted handcart he plied in the streets on Saturdays. His father was cruel and beat him regularly in their backyard, where the ice-cream was churned every day and scraggy fowls looked frightened. Yet, always smiling, Aldo remained gay as his pink, blue and white cart, an example of triumphant manhood arrived at early fruit. He piled ice-cream extravagantly high in the halfpenny cornets, perhaps to spite his mean father. I much admired Aldo and, in the Italian way, he admired my admiration. His sister, about three years younger than him, must have been rising thirteen when I married her.

Idwal, an outwards-looking friend of mine at that time, married us. A leader in our school class, he always treated Vanna with the disinterested contempt of the 100 per cent extrovert; she was a tomboy, often joined in our street games, seemed to have no girl-friends but owned a skipping rope with wooden handles and, her

mane whirling, could skip a couple of hundred jumps without stopping. No doors opened into Idwal's granite heart for her or anyone else. He possessed natural authority, a finely soaring soprano voice and a talent for accurate mimicry of grown men and women. He wore a surplice in St Thomas's church choir, and for the event in the coke oven on a quiet August holiday afternoon he smuggled this out of his home, where his mother had given it its monthly washing and starching. Garbed in it, he fixed rimless pince-nez on the tip of his nose. Four boxes formed an altar. On it stood a bottle of ginger pop Vanna had stolen from her parents' shop, a Church of England prayer book and a Christmas cracker ring which had a blue stone.

Vanna spread a lacy handkerchief over her hair. Idwal, standing before the altar, stopped her giggles with a forbidding squint above the pince-nez. It should have been a warning to me of their confederacy. I was not really a school dunce or entirely retarded, but I was not as bright as Idwal, though my eyes saw more than his. Opening the prayer book, he looked serious as a funeral and his soprano took on a deep underswell. He did not intone all the marriage service, and since I did not know the ceremony then, I could not suspect that this scampering had a motive.

'You put the ring on her finger now, boy *bach,*' he censured me. 'Pay attention.'

The ring on, he blessed us from the prayer book, took a first long swig from the bottle and passed it to us. 'I'll keep guard outside the door,' he promised, pulling his surplice off and removing his pince-nez. 'If it's two whistles there's someone coming.' Vanna's short neck swelled thick as she swallowed a bride's mouthful of pop, then passed the bottle to me. Outside, Idwal gave the iron door a shove, closing it as far as it could go on its broken hinges. Sufficient light came from a chink there, and from under the loose zinc sheet covering the hole in the roof, for me to see a gleam in Vanna's dancing eye. Looking round at me, she put a knee on the altar. She lay full length on it and whipped up the front of her frock. She wore no drawers. I saw the forbidden mystery. It was like a dusky apricot.

There was an ugly clatter. A shaft of hard daylight flooded the oven. The sheet of corrugated zinc had been hurled aside. A face lay over the edge of the hole. 'Hey, what d'you think you're doing down there?' The guttural voice cracked. 'Sergeant Richards here!' The face vanished. 'Get the handcuffs on him, Jenkins.' I had tumbled on to the ground. Vanna's squeal as she had leapt up was as unnerving. She pushed the door half open and ran. By the time I scrambled up and got outside she had rounded the row of ovens. Idwal, hands on hips, stood grinning cynically, on the bank above. 'No good chasing her, boy *bach*. Legs like a whippet's.' He leapt down. 'Better than a game of marbles, eh?'

Yet I did not feel I had been fooled; I even felt well-disposed towards Idwal, although somewhere inside myself I also began to reject him. That same week, as if I had provided *him* with pleasure, he gave me a bull's-eye marble, and, to my surprise, he did not gab about the coke oven event to schoolfriends. Vanna's conduct became as strange. She ignored me after our marriage. I vainly sought opportunity to speak to her. When we passed in the main street, almost every day, her gaze became fixed on her lifted nose. Even more surprisingly, she did not join us again in our back-lane games — she used to play marbles with us, squatting beside the marked ring like a boy. A Catholic, she attended a tin church in Tonypandy which had been built for the poor Irish immigrants who sought a less hard life in the Rhondda. I had heard that Catholics rid themselves of anything nasty by kneeling before a priest in a cupboard. Had Vanna confessed her marriage and been forbidden to associate with me? A few months after the marriage she put her hair up, much earlier in life than was the practice of Welsh girls. Then suddenly I saw her no more in the street.

'Where's Vanna gone?' I asked my brother-in-law one day, across the handcart. I felt I had a right to ask.

'Italy.' Aldo's smile at me, because it was perpetual, had no significance. But he had given me a quick glance. 'Turin. With our Grandmother. Not coming back.' Licking my cornet, I lingered in dissatisfaction. He took up the cart-handles and trundled off without another word to me.

***

A Child's Christmas in Wales

In one of his best-known pieces of prose, Dylan Thomas draws on his Swansea childhood in a typically vivid, freewheeling way.

One Christmas was so much like another, in those years around the sea-town corner now and out of all sound except the distant speaking of the voices I sometimes hear a moment before sleep, that I can never remember whether it snowed for six days and six nights when I was twelve or whether it snowed for twelve days and twelve nights when I was six. All the Christmases roll down toward the two-tongued sea, like a cold and headlong moon bundling down the sky that was our street; and they stop at the rim of the ice-edged fish-freezing waves, and I plunge my hands in the snow and bring out whatever I can find. In goes my hand into that wool-white bell-tongued ball of holidays resting at the rim of the carol-singing sea, and out come Mrs. Prothero and the firemen.

It was on the afternoon of the day of Christmas Eve, and I was in Mrs. Prothero's garden, waiting for cats, with her son Jim. It was snowing. It was always snowing at Christmas. December, in my memory, is white as Lapland, though there were no reindeers. But there were cats. Patient, cold and callous, our hands wrapped in socks, we waited to snowball the cats. Sleek and long as jaguars and horrible-whiskered, spitting and snarling, they would slink and sidle over the white back-garden walls, and the lynx-eyed hunters, Jim and I, fur-capped and moccasined trappers from Hudson Bay, off Mumbles Road, would hurl our deadly snowballs at the green of their eyes. The wise cats never appeared. We were so still, Eskimo-footed arctic marksmen in the muffling silence of the eternal snows — eternal, ever since Wednesday — that we never heard Mrs. Prothero's first cry from her igloo at the bottom of the garden. Or, if we heard it at all, it was, to us, like the far-off challenge of our enemy and prey, the neighbour's polar cat. But soon the voice grew louder.

'Fire!' cried Mrs. Prothero, and she beat the dinner-gong.

And we ran down the garden, with the snowballs in our arms, toward the house; and smoke, indeed, was pouring out of the dining-room and the bong was bombilating, and Mrs. Prothero was announcing ruin like a town crier in Pompeii. This was better than all the cats in Wales standing on the wall in a row. We bounded into the house, laden with snowballs, and stopped at the open door of the smoke-filled room. Something was burning all right; perhaps it was Mr. Prothero, who always slept there after midday dinner with a

newspaper over his face. But he was standing in the middle of the room, saying, 'A fine Christmas!' and smacking at the smoke with a slipper.

'Call the fire brigade,' cried Mrs. Prothero as she beat the gong.

'They won't be there,' said Mr. Prothero, 'it's Christmas.'

There was no fire to be seen, only clouds of smoke and Mr. Prothero standing in the middle of them, waving his slipper as though he were conducting.

'Do something,' he said.

And we threw all our snowballs into the smoke — I think we missed Mr. Prothero — and ran out of the house to the telephone box.

'Let's call the police as well,' Jim said.

'And the ambulance.'

'And Ernie Jenkins, he like fires.'

But we only called the fire brigade, and soon the fire engine came and three tall men in helmets brought a hose into the house and Mr. Prothero got out just in time before they turned it on. Nobody could have had a noiser Christmas Eve. And when the fireman turned off the hose and were standing in the wet, smoky room, Jim's aunt, Miss Prothero, came downstairs and peered in at them. Jim and I waited, very quietly, to hear what she would say to them. She said the right thing, always. She looked at the three tall firemen in their shining helmets, standing among the smoke and cinders and dissolving snowballs, and she said: 'Would you like anything to read?'

***

Ash On a Young Man's Sleeve

The writer Dannie Abse's autobiographical novel records his early life in Cardiff. Later he was to study medicine before qualifying as a doctor in London. In this extract though, that still lies ahead of the daydreaming adolescent as he leaves the hospital where he's been visiting Nancy Roberts with two other friends, Keith and Lydia. (Leo is his brother, and Grynszpan a young Jewish assassin who avenged the death of his parents in 1938.)

We left the ward solemnly; glad to leave its formality, glad to quit the mansions of the sick and old. Down the whirring lift through the faint ether-odour of the Casualty Department into the street of many colours. Outside the hospital stood a white ambulance. The flower woman still stood there smiling, and a student passed us with a stethoscope conspicuously sticking out of his pocket. Keith nearly bumped into a man who stared at the doors of the hospital vacantly, afraid perhaps to go in.

We accompanied Lydia home, up the hill, talking and dreaming. Between fragments of conversation I saw myself, self looking upon another self — and that other, a white-gowned, white-masked surgeon. I had recurrent daydreams of myself playing cricket for Glamorgan, scoring the winning goal for Cardiff City, or agitating a responsive crowd, like Leo did, demanding a Government of the People, for the People. Sometimes I imagined myself as another Grynszpan. But now, looking down at the haggard patient before self's other eyes, I saw that reclining figure assume the familiar features of Nancy Roberts. I said to the beautiful brunette nurse, 'This is inoperable, I will operate.' Only a gasp of amazement and admiration disturbed the silence of the operating room. The anaesthetic bag inflated and collapsed, inflated and collapsed as Nancy Roberts stood on the threshold of 'Life' and 'Death'.

'We must save the life of Nancy Roberts,' I said to the nurse who looked like Kay Francis.

'Impossible,' she answered. 'Even you couldn't do it.' The breathing continued, diminished; the spectators in the gallery clenched their fists until their knuckles turned white.

' I must try,' I said modestly. 'Now pass me more blood.'

They brought me a bottle of red fluid.

'No,' I said, 'the green blood.'

'Green?' they asked, surprised.

'Yes,' I commanded. 'Blood saturated with chlorophyll. It's the only way to save Nancy Roberts.'

'Where shall we get it?' they queried.

I took the syringe and needle, sticking it into one of my own veins, and the green corpuscles trickled out, remarkably. When I completed the operation the bladder of air expanded rapidly.

'There you are,' I said. 'Next patient.'

'Don't work any more today,' pleaded a blonde nurse. 'You've been operating twenty-four hours solid, without food, without water, without sleep.'

'I'll take a glass of water,' I remarked. 'The rest can wait. You must not put self first in a profession like ours.'

'Sir,' said the Kay Francis nurse, 'the next operation is on a man called Keith Thomas — cancer of the brain.'

'Wheel him in,' I sighed.

At the gate of the house we said good-bye to Lydia Pike, and Keith and I walked down Penylan Hill again.

'You've been very quiet,' said Keith.

'I've been thinking,' I said.

'What?' he asked.

'I think I'll become a doctor after all.'

'Thought you were going to be a poet and an assassin,' Keith reminded me.

'No,' I said, 'One must choose the difficult path. It's too easy to be a poet, or to knock off a few heads of Europe. Too easy. I'll take the difficult path. Anyway, I believe in Democracy.'

'What'll you be tomorrow?' smiled Keith.

'Dunno,' I said.

***

Discussion

Having read the three previous passages by Rhys Davies, Dylan Thomas and Dannie Abse, think about what the writers suggest about childhood in general, choosing one of the following subjects: innocence, friendship, fantasy. Make a list of points for discussion.

*

Is there one sentence or paragraph that you remember as being especially vivid so far? Why?

Tide-Race

Brenda Chamberlain was born in Bangor, north Wales, and trained as a painter at the Royal Academy in London. For fourteen years she lived on Bardsey Island. Her autobiographical Tide-Race records the last days of a small island community.

A few days before Christmas, a child died. Somewhere in the world an infant dies every hour; but not within living memory had a baby died here; so its death was more than usually calamitous.

Dic Longshanks and his wife already had four children; the eldest not yet five years old when the fifth was born. No sooner had one been born than the next had been conceived. It was a hard life for Leah, being tied to a primitive farmhouse, with babies tumbling about her feet wherever she moved. She had no escape, no relaxation. Dic, being of a roving, unstable disposition, liked the freedom of the place, for here he was his own master; whereas on the mainland, he would have been a farm servant or a road-mender.

A sign that disaster was coming to the farm Clogwyn had been given the previous summer, leaving the mark of ill-omen on the house. A few days after it had been stacked, Dic had had the misfortune to lose his hay by fire; the rick bursting into flame without apparent cause.

Dic and the other men were out on the sea lifting their lobster pots when the hay began to smoulder.

Leah, who was seven months heavy with child, on going out at the back door to fetch water from the well, saw a red tongue lick out from the side of the stack. She shut the children in the house, and hurried to Ty Draw, to get help from her sister.

It was some time before the men saw the cloud of smoke rising from the middle of the island. They were just in time to save a little of the hay by dousing the flames with buckets of water carried from the well in the mountain.

Dic's eyes had a haunted look in them after the fire had been put out. We stood resting, our hands and faces streaked with dirt, beside the stinking wreck of the haystack. He must have been thinking as most of us were of an old saying. It was Cadwaladr who put the thoughts into words as those of us who lived in the north were walking home.

'If hay goes on fire at ebb tide, it will bring bad luck to the farmer. If it burns at the flood, it will bring the man good luck.'

The hay had gone on fire as the tide was falling.

Months after, one breakfast time on a morning in late December,

Dic came round to tell us that his youngest baby (the one Leah had been carrying inside her at the time of the fire) had died in the blackness before dawn.

This was on a Friday, after a night of storm with fierce gusts from the east leaping the mountain top to batter the houses. Scarcely any of us had slept peacefully that night. Doors had burst open and buckets had flown over the ground. The baby had been sickly for a fortnight, but not ill enough to make his parents uneasy.

Dic and Leah had sat with the baby by the kitchen fire, not understanding that it was about to die. The breath left it a little after six o'clock in the morning. The body weighed less at death than at birth; the limbs were quite shrunken, no bigger than a doll's, and the face was blue and green and sharp as a bird's.

When it grew light, the father came round the island with the news. It was too late to fetch a doctor, and the heavy seas made it impossible for one of our small boats to cross for the coroner. Dic went up to the lighthouse and had a message sent over the radio telegraph to the coastguard forty miles away. The coastguard then telephoned the message to our nearest mainland village with the news.

The sea was hungry; the noise of it had hurt our ears for days. Huge foam-crested waves broke on one another's backs in their haste to pass our shores.

On Saturday afternoon, permission was received by wireless for the child to be buried without an inquest. After the message came, three amateur grave-diggers went by on the path, through the incessant grey downpouring of rain. The men were tall and black in rain-sodden oilskins and sea boots. Each man carried a spade over his shoulder. They were Dic, his brother-in-law Jacob, and the sea-wrinkled Cadwaladr.

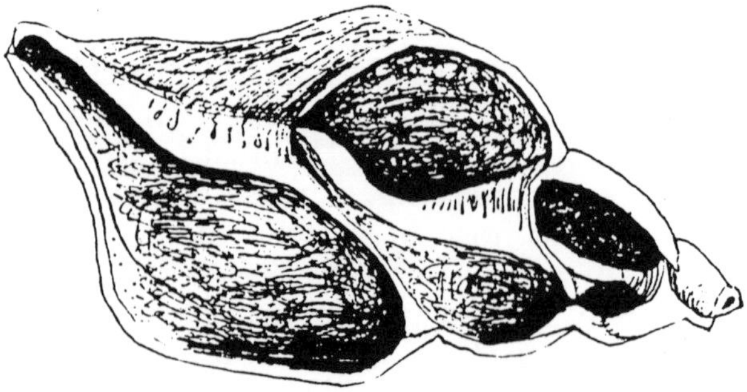

There was a pale exhausted light in the sky after days and nights of storm. A heavy swell was breaking against the back cliffs. The men spent the afternoon in the graveyard, digging a deep hole. Meanwhile, Bill Levens was making a coffin out of driftwood. When the box was finished, he darkened it with floor stain, and fitted a leather strap handle at either end. On the lid he screwed small pieces of copper in the form of a cross.

Soon after dark on Sunday, the evening before the funeral, Bill Levens and his wife and one or two others went to Dic's, to take away the body.

'Where have you put the corpse?' asked Mrs. Levens. Leah went to the dresser, the middle drawer of which was locked. Turning a key in it, she opened the drawer, saying:

'There was nowhere else to put it, to have it out of the hands of the children. They kept wanting to play with it.'

The Levens's fought their way back through driving rain and darkness to the chapel that had not been used for five or six years. After they had arranged the corpse in the fragile coffin, they placed it beside the altar for the night.

We buried the child next day. Soon after breakfast, I saw Dic passing up the lane. A little later, he returned carrying in his hand a pair of shining Sunday boots. He had borrowed a suit and boots from Owain in order to appear respectable at the funeral, for he had nothing of his own to wear except his ragged fishing clothes.

Around eleven o'clock, two lightkeepers joined the chief islander at the door of his workshop; after them, came the bereaved parents. They were followed by Jacob and Eira.

In the sun and wind that made of the water green and purple meadows, a wine-dark Odyssean sea, eleven of us gathered in the chapel.

The children had been left at home in charge of Rhiannon. We scarcely knew one another in our best clothes. The patriarchal figure in the wide-brimmed black hat, looking like a preacher, was Cadwaladr.

My god, Cadwaladr in mourning!

Black tie, white collar, a dark suit, and a hat like a sombrero.

Feet shuffled on the tiled floor of the mildew-smelling chapel. The service, which only lasted a few minutes, was conducted by the Ancient Mariner, who read a few short prayers, hurrying over them, for he was unnerved by the terrible sobbing of the mother. We did not sing; it being winter, there were no flowers. We could not trust ourselves to sing; and there were no flowers in December.

We filed out into the weak sunlight, past the ruined tower of the abbey to the grave that was already half-full of clay-coloured water.

The doll-coffin was lowered on a thick white cord. In the west corner of the graveyard, an effigy of an angel stood in solitude, holding out her arms to the whirlpools and twisting currents below. She was marble, and a prisoner in a whitewashed wire cage.

Poor angel! I had several times tried to force the padlock chaining the gate to an iron upright at one of the corners. I had never succeeded in opening it, and had always had to walk away, pretending a detachment; walking carefully between the sarcophagi and the drunken headstones; saying to myself:

'She is only a marble effigy, and they have put a wire net over the creature so the gulls may not soil her garments and wings.'

But that was a terrible thought. Not even the birds might touch her. There were always refinements to horror; one day, a wren had found its way through the mesh and was beating itself to death in attempts to get out again.

'Here lies the child Ianto who will never sail the summer seas, nor with his father fish for fine lobster, nor know the dangers of winter in the Sound.'

***

Walking the Plank

In this autobiographical essay, Janice Short, who works as a tree-feller, describes her experience as an English woman coming to live in Dyfed, among the Preseli mountains.

The valley behind the chapel is alive tonight with the whooping of mating owls. It's mild and very dark, a soft, deep, living black. An owl calls restlessly near the house and is answered by a tumult of tremulous hoots from the wooded valley in the middle distance. There is a track there which I followed one day until it led me into an impassable marsh. In the bottom runs the stream which also flows past the vestry. It's very loud tonight, with a deep, glooping undernote, a swallowing sound, turbulent and powerful. The owl calls and calls. Somewhere in the cry is a human sound. It's saying something. Abandoned valley alive with the voices of owls. Deserted cottage in the woods and the little farm all overgrown with bramble and laurel where I saw the fox slip away in the long wet grass in the rain. I stood outside in the patch of light that falls across the grass from the window. Across the rhythm of my own breathing, felt rather than heard, was another.

Two years and three months. That's how long it is since I came to Wales.

Watching snowflakes slanting past a green wall of spruce. Burrowing into the piles of dry brush, ferreting in my satchel for the life-giving flask, easing off my felling mitt to nurse the hot plastic cup. Peering from under my dripping visor at the softened outline of the mountain with a curious sense of security and well-being. That was the first winter. I didn't know I was in Wales, then, though I suspected something.

Night again, now. A dirty, wild night. The mock spring of this morning was in some other world. Tonight I know I'm in Wales, but I'm uneasy. Caught between two worlds. I don't want to fall down the crack in between. I wanted to simplify my life but it's not simple now.

That old tree of knowledge, still going strong and chucking a spanner in the works.

Why didn't I know I was in Wales that first year? Because I didn't know what Wales was. I didn't know what England was when I lived there, either. It's not just that history was badly taught in that secondary school in the south Yorkshire hills with the smudgy reek of Sheffield on the horizon. What they taught us wasn't history. British history, my history, centuries and centuries of it, had simply been gouged away, leaving a raw, gaping hole, like the one which used to be the garden of Ty Capel. Instead, a truncated and unconvincing sketch of Anglo-Saxons in thonged leggings and Willie the Conk. Before that — dinosaurs. No wonder I was bored and restless, and never really enjoyed the beautiful hill country that surrounded my early home. There was always something missing.

Settled in my deep armchair by the Rayburn on an afternoon that is noticeably longer and lighter, and the outside sounds, a coal-tit calling, the lowing of Elgan's cows, voices and distant activity from the farm all have a more open, carrying quality. Surely it's not spring yet? But this morning after a perilous descent down the slippery face of the pit and a bloody and inconclusive clash with the brambles, I picked a small handful of daffodils, just out. Then I went to help Gwen Jones to light her coal fire. When I gave her the lilies she kissed them. Gwen lived in Ty Capel for twenty-seven years, and it was not she who carried off the topsoil when she left.

That winter Gwen started teaching me Welsh by that fire, with the aid of a hymn-book and the annual chapel report. We had the television on with the sound down unless something interesting came on. I wanted the Welsh programmes, but Gwen is addicted to Les Dawson and 'The Price is Right'. She told me of her life in Ty Capel. Less than twenty years ago it was still a full-time job, the best bedroom always reserved and kept aired for if the minister needed to stay. There were functions most nights in the vestry that is too big and too cold, now, for the handful of children who attend Sunday School. In the lane, close to the chapel, is a row of weavers' cottages. They used to be called 'The Street'. When there was a wedding in the chapel the inhabitants of the Street decorated their cottages inside and out. Flowers spilled into the lane from the gardens and window-boxes, children played in the brook. The last inhabitant of the Street, Bessie, went to stay with her daughter-in-law a few weeks ago.

Bessie is ill. Her son still goes to the cottage to light a fire and feed the cats but we know, though it's never said, that she isn't coming back. All the other cottages are holiday homes.

*

It's very silent. I'm sitting with my coat on, writing, late at night. Silence rings in my ears. Only the occasional faint tick from the smouldering log in the cooling Rayburn. It's neither spring nor winter.

The year is turning.

When I first knew the village I thought that Welsh and English cultures were blended. I saw my mistake after a while, and it seems incredible to me now that I could have arrived with such depleted awareness. What is wrong in England that promotes a state of complete ignorance about part of the island we're living on? The two cultures operate alongside but do not touch. Having gathered enough Welsh to be able to read a simple poster — that's the first step — I went to a *Noson Lawen*. I had been in the place before. I'd seen many of the people before and spoken with some of them. I know that everyone would be speaking Welsh. But I was totally unprepared for the experience of immersion in an atmosphere where Welsh was dominant. The language is central but it's not just the language. It was like being plunged suddenly into another medium, and I floundered like a landed halibut. The other people in the room were patient, courteous, humorous. It's often a wonder to me how they can remain so.

'They're terribly rude, you know...' say English friends — nice people, really. It confuses and disturbs me. How can it be rude to speak Welsh in Wales? Is it arrogance, ignorance, fear, in the people who talk this way? Not in the ones I'm thinking of. It's just an incurable blindness, and it makes me restless and sad.

Gone, now, are the days of innocence, when I gained new words every day and brought them out in shops and pubs and practised on my neighbours. Struggling on the greasy upward slope of the see-saw, I think I'll never reach the magic fulcrum in the middle. Will I ever be able to take the step that will tip me into that other medium — a sort of linguistic walking the plank? A friend in the Welsh class tells me he dreams in Welsh, now. I'm not a jealous person but I could have kicked him.

Susannah went into hospital this morning and I'd promised to take the cat. When I went to see her she was in her dressing gown, awaiting the ambulance in her sway-backed cottage under the oaks, in its acre of wilderness. Snowdrops round the ash heap, comfrey springing up through the framework of an old sofa, heaven knows what in the rotting railway shed against the hedge. Soon the primroses will be out again under the oaks. Susannah is afraid of the oaks. She's afraid of many things. But when she lifted her wan face I knew she was good for another ten years. The tragedy is that I had to ask myself if that's a good thing.

Shipwrecked lives. Susannah has travelled the world but learned nothing, now clinging to the flotsam of the past, adrift on a hostile current. It is not love of life that will keep her alive but the fear of death. She can't come to terms with either. Gwen, who is frightened of the real sea, steers her vessel skilfully by the lights she has always known. When the time comes she will recognize her harbour and enter it in peace. Her chief navigator has always been her heart.

I didn't realize I'd started to change until I left. A matter of a mile, no more. A mile, a world away. I soon found out. For the first time I'd known personal identification with a physical part of the earth's crust, a specific configuration of skyline and stars, shadow and light, and what it is to separate from it. In Welsh, there is a word. *Hiraeth*. There's no complete equivalent in English.

***

Discussion

The writers of the two previous passages, Brenda Chamberlain and Janice Short, are outsiders describing the experience of places new to them. In what ways are their experiences different?

*

To which of these places could you adapt better? What about them seems to you attractive, what unattractive?

In The Night

Childhood bed
Like a bough on the windy night,
Rain beating and pit grinding,
Trucks banging together,
Far down over the fields.

I could not sleep without the brutality
Of the night voices,
Not for many years.

In summer, early,
Hearing sheep
Thud past the fence, for shearing
The smell of wool, the lost cries...

Out of dream, sometimes,
connecting the crake of a drawer
Full of odds and ends, with a long hooting.
Why? Never sorted — but it raised fears.
I would lift the curtain
To see Rhondda fixed on the dark,
A throw of stars.

Jean Earle

Suggestions

Oral

Which did you find the most interesting piece of autobiography, and which the least? Why?

'To know me now you should have known me in my childhood.' Is that true of you?

If two or three members of the class were prepared to be interviewed about their lives by the rest, a chairperson could control the flow of questions. (Or the interviewees could assume the roles of well-known people answering questions as in a chat show.)

Writing

Organising your ideas beforehand, and writing as interestingly as you can, choose one of these subjects on which to write:

a) For several writers — Dylan Thomas and Emlyn Williams, for instance — people haunt their memories. Which people figure most largely in yours?

b) Keep a diary for a week, including observations about other people as well as yourself, and keeping sharp eyes (and ears) open.

c) 'The truth is, of course, that there is no pure truth, only the separate accounts of witnesses,' Laurie Lee has written about autobiography. Can you think of any incident(s) in your life which someone else who was there would record differently?

d) Brenda Chamberlain recalls an especially dramatic episode in her life on Bardsey Island. What's the most dramatic thing (it might have seemed so to you and no one else) that you have experienced so far?

e) Questions about the past (Who am I? What have I become?) bring with them an unspoken question about the future: What might I become? What might you become?

Places

Words in Focus

Several writers in the first section, on autobiography, recalled the importance to them of their birthplaces, the first scenes they knew. But places we value needn't be those we have lived in. A beach glimpsed from a train, a street where you often visited an aunt, a cave you once explored on holiday — such places have the power to haunt.

Driving in Fog

Driving in fog I part the crowded air,
Then the night falls huge and white across the car.

It is as if I stopped believing in the world
The dark conceals, preferring the immense, cold

Flowerings of fog the headlights stain
To dull amber, the solderings of rain

That glisten on the crawling vehicle.
Yet I never seem to break its streaming wall,

Never reach that moment I can rightly say
Here it begins: always it remains a yard away

In the blurred crowding of fields that overhang
The road, the pale entangling yarns

Of my own breath. Here is not the rain's
Assault, the sullen-strange communion

Of the snow. This is no weather but the bland
Present's arrest, for even the trees stand

Like inked letters half-erased. All traffic
Stops. The fog's white sweat gives radiance to the dark.

In a shrunken world I wait for it to pass,
But the fog like countless faces crowds the glass.

Robert Minhinnick

Discussion

Perhaps the importance of our places, our miniature worlds, can be judged best by imagining their opposite. What would placelessness be like? With no real point of contact with what's around us? It would be, says the poet in 'Driving in Fog', a 'shrunken world', as if we'd 'stopped believing in the world'. More generally, it's what would happen if we lived with only a dim sense of where we are, its rustling present and half-buried past. Frozen in time, the driver can only watch the fog, wait for it to pass. But he is fully alert. A good writer is someone on whom nothing is wasted. What do the first and last lines have in common?

*

Robert Minhinnick uses visual images to catch the experience for the reader to share. He shows us rather than just tells us. Some images explain themselves, simple facts: the car, its headlights, the fields. Others, though, compare two things using 'like' or 'as'. Called similes (as in 'similar'), they crop up often in our everyday conversation: 'He went as white as a sheet'. But a writer needs to invent fresh comparisons, to give new life to old words. 'The fog like countless faces crowds the glass', pressing in on the driver starved of company. Why does the poet think that the trees 'look like letters half-erased'?

*

More often, the poet makes sudden comparisons which sidestep 'like' and 'as'. Rather than writing that the fog is 'like an immense cold flowering', he mentions 'the immense cold flowering' of fog. Such a strange white blooming around the car. That's a metaphor, and we use metaphor whenever we say that someone looks sour, or promise to turn over a new leaf, or complain that a baby is screaming its head off. They're not literally true, these comparisons, but they're useful ways of picturing ideas. Which of these metaphors in 'Driving in Fog' can you picture most vividly?

I *part* the crowded air

its streaming *wall*

yarns/ of my own breath

the fog's white *sweat*

The River and the Road

The moon too has her times:
Last night
I was alone at the old bridge watching her at it,
Flinging into the swirling flood
Plate after white plate,
Recklessly smashing them all:
Each fragment giddily swimming a moment
Before sinking:
Then another,
And another.

When I turned from the bridge,
The moon was on the road:
She had now forgotten her mad prank at the river
And was pensively walking ahead of me:
Carefully, lovingly she picked up,
As if it had been a jewel,
Every bit of jagged flint
And the tiniest pieces of broken glass.

Wil Ifan

Discussion

Think about which metaphor you prefer in each pair of brackets:

> The streets were still. In the distance, a church spire (bridged/spiked) the clouds. Then a wind sprang up, (whipping/ hammering) the leaves, spinning them. Clouds were (pockets/ bruises) in the evening sky.

Now look again at the poet's metaphor about plates. He could have written that, instead of flinging white plates into the river, the moon threw parcels. For which reasons are plates better?

*

What does the simile at the end of the poem suggest to you?

*

As well as simile and metaphor, there's a third kind of comparison. To compare something with a person is to use personification — a plant looks sad, say, or a chair groans under someone's weight. It's a connection that, even when it's not really new, gives energy to what we say. But ideally it should be new. This poet, for example, has seen the river in a new light. Which words in 'The River and the Road' suggest that the moon is human and has moods? ('Pensively,' for instance, means 'thoughtfully'.) And why does her mood change in the second section?

*

Try writing a brief description — a poem if you like — in which you personify a mountain, a building, the sea or...Choose something you know.

Foghorns

When Catrin was a small child
She thought the foghorn moaning
Far out at sea was the sad
Solitary voice of the moon
Journeying to England.
She heard it warn 'Moon, Moon',
As it worked the Channel, trading
Weather like rags and bones.

Tonight, after the still sun
And the silent heat, as haze
Became rain and weighed glistening
In brimful leaves, and the last bus
Splashes and fades with a soft
Wave-sound, the foghorns moan, moon-
Lonely and the dry lawns drink.
This dimmed moon, calling still,
Hauls sea-rags through the streets.

Gillian Clarke

The Fog Horn

In this soup thick night, the fog horn
Calls, like a cow in pain
Sounding its lonely rhythms. Its long

Notes travel not only the sea's swell, but
Float over fields full of sleeping cattle, then
To towns, through deserted streets,
Pulsing through my window, reaching

My ears. How many people listen,
Lying in their beds awake
To the soft displacement of silence.

Like hearing a dying animal,
It proves that yet a life exists
Marking the human shorelines
With its pulse.

And all around the sea
Stretches, falling over the horizon's rims.

Frances Williams

Discussion

Apart from the foghorns, what else do the poems have in common?

*

The foghorn in the first poem has a human voice, the one in the second an animal's. What difference does that make?

*

Why did each poet use words with 's' sounds to accompany the word 'soft' in each poem, do you think? (See line thirteen in the first poem, and line ten in the second.)

*

Look at the longest sentence in each poem, beginning 'Tonight' and 'Its long'. Considering what these sentences describe, do you find it right that they should be long?

*

Each poem ends with a metaphor. Which one do you prefer? And which poem did you prefer overall? Why?

Voices

Swonzee Boy See?

Sorrite livin up ere
bi farout like f ew wannoo gerrin t town.
Yea I knowzits er city
burile olliz call it town.

I wuz born downer Sandfields see,
down by werra Soshull is now
— eza joke forew.

Ayve done some fancy work round air, avenay?
Sorl been tarted up like
round byer Lehjha un South Dock.
Ew doan see flats like at up Blineymice.
Meenmy brother ewsed t dive inner dock
— few tryed it now ewed crack ew ed onner yot.

I been in at Marrytime Museyum.
Ayve got bit vunole Mumbles train air.
I remember at wen I wozer kid.
Ewsed t put apenees onner line
forrer trains to go overum
soze ayde ged as big as pennys —
try um inner chewing gum machines see?

Awler famly ewsed t go downer Bracelet inner summer
on at ole train—
evenee ole man.
Ew could mover seats
soze ew coudall sitagether.

Ay still maker lotter fuss bout at train
ewed think it wuzy ony thing ut ad been taken from air.

David Hughes

What Can You Give Me?

O what can you give me?
Say the sad bells of Rhymney.

Is there hope for the future?
Cry the brown bells of Merthyr.

Who made the mineowner?
Say the black bells of Rhondda.

And who robbed the miner?
Cry the grim bells of Blaina.

They will plunder willy-nilly,
Say the bells of Caerphilly.

They have fangs, they have teeth!
Shout the loud bells of Neath.

To the south, things are sullen,
Say the pink bells of Brecon.

Even God is uneasy,
Say the moist bells of Swansea.

Put the vandals in court!
Cry the bells of Newport.

All would be well if - if- if-
Say the green bells of Cardiff.

Why so worried, sisters, why?
Sing the silver bells of Wye.

Idris Davies

The Collier

When I was born on Amman hill
A dark bird crossed the sun.
Sharp on the floor the shadow fell;
I was the youngest son.

And when I went to the County School
I worked in a shaft of light.
In the wood of the desk I cut my name:
Dai for Dynamite.

The tall black hills my brothers stood;
Their lessons all were done.
From the door of the school when I ran out
They frowned to watch me run.

The slow grey bells they rung a chime
Surly with grief or age.
Clever or clumsy, lad or lout,
All would look for a wage.

I learnt the valley flowers' names
And the rough bark knew my knees.
I brought home trout from the river
And spotted eggs from the trees.

A coloured coat I was given to wear
Where the lights of the rough land shone.
Still jealous of my favour
The tall black hills looked on.

They dipped my coat in the blood of a kid
And they cast me down a pit,
And although I crossed with strangers
There was no way up from it.

Soon as I went from the County School
I worked in a shaft. Said Jim,
'You will get your chain of gold, my lad,
But not for a likely time.'

And one said, 'Jack was not raised up
When the wind blew out the light
Though he interpreted their dreams
And guessed their fears by night.'

And Tom, he shivered his leper's lamp
For the stain that round him grew;
And I heard mouths pray in the after-damp
When the picks would not break through.

They changed words there in darkness
And still through my head they run,
And white on my limbs is the linen sheet
And gold on my neck the sun.

Vernon Watkins

Synopsis of the Great Welsh Novel

Dai K lives at the end of a valley. One is not quite sure
Whether it has been drowned or not. His Mam
Loves him too much and his Dada drinks.
As for his girlfriend Blodwen, she's pregnant. So
Are all the other girls in the village — there's been a Revival.
After a performance of Elijah, the mad preacher
Davies the Doom has burnt the chapel down.
One Saturday night after the dance at the Con Club,
With the Free Wales Army up to no good in the back lanes,
A stranger comes to the village; he is, of course,
God, the well known television personality. He succeeds
In confusing the issue, whatever it is, and departs
On the last train before the line is closed.
The colliery blows up, there is a financial scandal
Involving all the most respected citizens; the Choir
Wins at the National. It is all seen, naturally,
Through the eyes of a sensitive boy who never grows up.
The men emigrate to America, Cardiff and the moon. The girls
Find rich and foolish English husbands. Only daft Ianto
Is left to recite the Complete Works of Sir Lewis Morris
To puzzled sheep, before throwing himself over
The edge of the abandoned quarry. One is not quite sure
Whether it is fiction or not.

Harri Webb

Before the Crying Ends

There being nothing special much around this town. Not like London nor Paris nor Rome nor Lisbon nor Washington. Not like Cardiff nor Tenby nor Bangor nor plenty of towns you can see anywhere.

No one particular item making you sit up sudden like you never believed what you saw first time off. Not a single special thing for making passing (on to God knows where) stangers remember where they been. No special beauty. No special ugliness. No sudden visions. And no sudden blindness as ever they (them passing stangers) could recall.

Nothing special much around this town for filling empty exiled nights and minds with nostalgia nor things hard to forget a hundred a thousand a hundred thousand miles away. Nothing memorable you understand. No one peculiar thing them passing eyes could retain for ever. No wide gasping geographical statement marked deep across the landscape making them (them passing strangers) whisper all holy:

Only God could have done that.

Now tell me there is no God.

God been poking his fingers up this place.

God definitely done that mountain (or that valley or that cliff or that forest or that sky).

Even the name of this place is forgettable. Pontypridd. A shambles of mystic Welshness. Pontypridd. Something to do with a bridge (there is a bridge). Pontypridd. Something to do with the earth (black stuff). Who could remember such a name? Who could care?

There being nothing special much around this town. Nothing at all. Except perhaps the river. Maybe just that.

The River Taff. Swilling down from Merthyr same as some kind of whip. Dirty candle-coloured by day down through Aberdare Mountain Ash Abercynon and Cilfynydd in a torrent. In a welter of torrents. Grunting sucking lashing whirlpools blackened through by mining trash and coal no man could burn.

Twisting fast down deep inside the guts of Pontypridd. Towards Cardiff. Carrying things. Always carrying things.

Dead terrier. Four headless chickens. Five loaves (from Wonderloaf) and two fish (from Plowman's) floating in circles amid surface scum just off that Marks and Spencer back wall. Two mangled oil cans from Texaco (by way of Halfords) and one sodden Western Mail hanging same as nests on the pea-shooter beds fringed haphazard around Ynysangharad Park. And a bucket. And a bugle. And a birthday card. And a trouser leg with the turn-up down. And a boy and his ferret hunting for rats.

Found a bike down there once.

Only needed a chain.

Found a chain down there once.

Only needed a bike.

And in flood that river is mighty. A frightening thing. Unstoppable (if ever man had a mind). Creaking heavy against them quaking banks where houses stand. And people stand. Staring. Up at the rain. Down at the river. Across at each other. Wondering. With tomboys chucking stones snick snick into the grey flow. And today it is raining as last night it rained and the day before. And the night before that day. For this town is Pontypridd. Where they know all about rain.

And it was raining when you got born. And it will be raining when you die. If you die in Pontypridd.

And mister I can tell you for nothing as how when that day comes you will definitely have enough on your plate working your dead mouth on a fiddle into Heaven never mind that hissing rain.

With thoughts like that definitely giving you the willies now and again seeing as how you are not ready for no bloody drop this fair side of three score years and ten. With a stack of functioning left for doing inside your skull not to mention all through your medium rare skin. Leaving them passing strangers to keep on passing by this forgettable place in a gust of wind and rain. On towards London or Paris or Rome or Lisbon or Washington or Cardiff or Tenby or Bangor or anywhere else. For this town is Pontypridd where the gods brought your soul at the beginning of time. And nailed it to the wall.

John L. Hughes

***

Discussion

'There being nothing special much around this town,' says John L. Hughes about Pontypridd, in one of the south Wales valleys. On the other hand, Harri Webb's poem 'Synopsis of the Great Welsh Novel' finds drama in the Valleys. What about the other two poems set in the Valleys, by Idris Davies and Vernon Watkins? What attitudes do they take?

*

And does the past in these writings have anything to say to (or about) our present?

*

Which lines or sentences so far in this section have stood out for their striking images?

Pwllcrochan

I spent weeks down here:
Spring and Autumn planting and picking,
thick wedges of bread and tea,
hands smelling of earth and potato juice;
story-book childhood weekends of stolen
apples, blown birds' eggs, trespassing;
rainy evenings exploring the smugglers' cellar,
shadows jerked alive by the throbbing light generator.

The Old Rectory has gone —
scraped flat for a Texaco car-park,
abandoned after six months.
Now, outbuildings enclose a grassy space,
an ache of absence.
We walk the rutted lake to the bay:
from the narrow, stone bridge inland
the refinery spreads its shining tentacles,
its waste-burner roaring, glowing through the day.

The small bay is thick with reeds, wiry grass:
stream trickling over wellington-hungry mud
to slide beneath shells and sandstone shale
into the once-secret Haven.
Across the deep water from our fishing rocks
the gantries suckle from fat tankers,
steel arteries pulse away through the hills.

Looking back up to the road
I frame you in the camera lens,
centred by the cleft of the sloping fields.
You turn, Gareth smiles in your arms
and the photo works perfectly,
bringing you into focus
and leaving all the rest behind.

As we walk back to the car, stepping from
bank to tussock, the marks of our weight in the mud stay,
draw an ooze of oil to rainbow our way.

Tony Curtis

On the Black Hill

For forty-two years, Lewis and Benjamin Jones slept side by side, in their parents' bed, at their farm which was known as 'The Vision'.

The bedstead, an oak four-poster, came from their mother's home at Bryn-Draenog when she married in 1899. Its faded cretonne hangings, printed with a design of larkspur and roses, shut out the mosquitoes of summer, and the draughts in winter. Calloused heels had worn holes in the linen sheets, and parts of the patchwork quilt had frayed. Under the goose-feather mattress, there was a second mattress, of horsehair, and this had sunk into two troughs, leaving a ridge between the sleepers.

The room was always dark and smelled of lavender and mothballs.

The smell of mothballs came from a pyramid of hatboxes piled up beside the washstand. On the bed-table lay a pincushion still stuck with Mrs Jones's hatpins; and on the end wall hung an engraving of Holman Hunt's 'Light of the World', enclosed in an ebonized frame.

One of the windows looked out over the green fields of England: the other looked back into Wales, past a clump of larches, at the Black Hill.

Both the brothers' hair was even whiter than the pillowcases.

Every morning their alarm went off at six. They listened to the farmers' broadcast as they shaved and dressed. Downstairs, they tapped the barometer, lit the fire and boiled a kettle for tea. Then they did the milking and foddering before coming back for breakfast.

The house had roughcast walls and a roof of mossy stone tiles and stood at the far end of the farmyard in the shade of an old Scots pine. Below the cowshed there was an orchard of wind-stunted apple-trees, and then the fields slanted down to the dingle, and there were birches and alders along the stream.

Long ago, the place had been called Ty-Cradoc — and Caractacus is still a name in these parts — but in 1737 an ailing girl called Alice Morgan saw the Virgin hovering over a patch of rhubarb, and ran back to the kitchen, cured. To celebrate the miracle, her father renamed his farm 'The Vision' and carved the initials A.M. with the date and a cross on the lintel above the porch. The border of Radnor and Hereford was said to run right through the middle of the staircase.

The brothers were identical twins.

As boys, only their mother could tell them apart: now age and accidents had weathered them in different ways.

Lewis was tall and stringy, with shoulders set square and a steady long-limbed stride. Even at eighty he could walk over the hills all day, or wield an axe all day, and not get tired.

He gave off a strong smell. His eyes — grey, dreamy and astygmatic — were set well back into the skull, and capped with thick round lenses in white metal frames. He bore the scar of a cycling accident on his nose and, ever since, its tip had curved downwards and turned purple in cold weather.

His head would wobble as he spoke: unless he was fumbling with his watch-chain, he had no idea what to do with his hands. In company he always wore a puzzled look; and if anyone made a statement of fact, he'd say, 'Thank you!' or 'Very kind of you!' Everyone agreed he had a wonderful way with sheepdogs.

Benjamin was shorter, pinker, neater and sharper-tongued. His chin fell into his neck, but he still possessed the full stretch of his nose, which he would use in conversation as a weapon. He had less hair.

He did all the cooking, the darning and the ironing; and he kept the accounts. No one could be fiercer in a haggle over stock-prices and he would go on, arguing for hours, until the dealer threw up his hands and said, 'Come off, you old skinflint!' and he'd smile and say, 'What can you mean by that?'

For miles around the twins had the reputation of being incredibly stingy — but this was not always so.

They refused, for example, to make a penny out of hay. Hay, they said, was God's gift to the farmer; and providing The Vision had hay to spare, their poorer neighbours were welcome to what they needed. Even in the foul days of January, old Miss Fifield the Tump had only to send a message with the postman, and Lewis would drive the tractor over with a load of bales.

Benjamin's favourite occupation was delivering lambs. All the long winter, he waited for the end of March, when the curlews started calling and the lambing began. It was he, not Lewis, who stayed awake to watch the ewes. It was he who would pull a lamb at a difficult birth. Sometimes, he had to thrust his forearm into the womb to disentangle a pair of twins; and afterwards, he would sit by the fireside, unwashed and contented, and let the cat lick the afterbirth off his hands.

In winter and summer, the brothers went to work in striped flannel shirts with copper studs to fasten them at the neck. Their jackets and waistcoats were made of brown whipcord, and their trousers were of darker corduroy. They wore their moleskin hats with the brims turned down; but since Lewis had the habit of lifting his to every stranger, his fingers had rubbed the nap off the peak.

From time to time, with a show of mock solemnity, they consulted their silver watches — not to tell the hour but to see whose watch was beating faster. On Saturday nights they took turns to have a hip-bath in front of the fire; and they lived for the memory of their mother.

Because they knew each other's thoughts, they even quarrelled without speaking. And sometimes — perhaps after one of these silent quarrels, when they needed their mother to unite them — they would stand over her patchwork quilt and peer at the black velvet stars and the hexagons of printed calico that had once been her dresses. And without saying a word they could see her again — in pink, walking through the oatfield with a jug of draught cider for the reapers. Or in green, at a sheep-shearers' lunch. Or in a blue-striped apron bending over the fire. But the black stars brought back a memory of their father's coffin, laid out on the kitchen table, and the chalk-faced women, crying.

Bruce Chatwin

***

The Chapel

A little aside from the main road,
becalmed in a last-century greyness,
there is the chapel, ugly, without the appeal
to the tourist to stop his car
and visit it. The traffic goes by,
and the river goes by, and quick shadows
of clouds, too, and the chapel settles
a little deeper into the grass.

But here once on an evening like this,
in the darkness that was about
his hearers, a preacher caught fire
and burned steadily before them
with a strange light, so that they saw
the splendour of the barren mountains
about them and sang their amens
fiercely, narrow but saved
in a way that men are not now.

R.S. Thomas

Above Penmaenmawr

The upland farmers have all gone;
the lane they laid twists without purpose,
visiting broken gates and overgrown
gardens, to end in clumps of gorse.

Their unroofed houses and fallen barns,
rich in nettles, lie dead in hiding
from the wind that howls off Talyfan's
saw-tooth ridge; their walls divide

bracken from bracken; their little church
of bare rock has outlasted use:
hikers' signatures in the porch,
'Keys obtainable at the Guesthouse'.

Yet, not to sentimentalize,
their faces turned from drudgery
when the chance showed itself. There is
hardly a sign of the husbandry

of even the last to leave — so slight
was their acceptance by the land.
They left for the seaside towns, to get
easier jobs, and cash in hand.

Five miles of uplands, and beyond —
a thousand feet below — the coast,
its bright lights twinkling; freezing wind
dragging the cloud down like a frost

from Talyfan. Alone upon
these darkening, silent heights, my fears
stay stubbornly with the farmers, gone
after six hundred thankless years.

Tony Connor

Summer in the Village

Now, you can see
where the widows live:
nettles grow tall and thistles seed
round old machinery.
Hayfields smooth under the scythe
simmer with tussocks;
the hedges begin to go,
and the bracken floods in.

Where the young folk have stayed on
gaudy crops of caravans
and tents erupt in the roadside fields;
Shell Gifts, Crab Sandwiches, To Let,
the signs solicit by the gates, left open
where the milk churns used to stand;
and the cash trickles in.

'For Sale' goes up again
on farms the townies bought with good intentions
and a copy of *The Whole Earth Guide;*
Samantha, Dominic and Willow play
among the geese and goats while parents in the pub
complain about Welsh education and the dole.
And a new asperity creeps in.

Now, you will see
the tidy management of second homes:
slightly startled, old skin stretched,
the cottages are made convenient.
There are boats with seats;
dogs with the work bred out of them
sit listlessly by garden chairs on Kodakcolor lawns;
and all that was community seeps out.

Christine Evans

Things to do when the town's closed

Our choir dressed as guerrilla butlers
has driven the holidaymakers back.
It is September. Seagulls
are critics prying over spilt ink.
The town's scraped off its silver lining
to get at the cloud instead.

In search of a bit of life,
Ron has started taxidermy, juggling
bags of skin like a homicidal vet.
They grin from furry cells,
near-squirrels.
You can't keep a good man up.

And Mr. S has emptied his firm's safe.
Self-bloodied, he faked
assault then described the villain
so well for the police photofit,
like a shout his own face rang out.

On the library wall: ANACKY.
Draughts from the Mersey Tunnel quicken
across the Dee. Wait,
slow down
at the station.
You can find yourself elsewhere.

Balloons were released in August
from Ffrith Beach for Holiday Fun
with addressed labels. W's returned
all the way from Builth. His prize?
First cash, soon a court appearance:

winds blew north that day so how come W's balloon
went south? Well, live in town
and wind is just a ghost. The label went
via his aunt in Builth, each way by post.

Yesterday, high on a ladder with acres
to paint, Mr. S was whistling *Born Free*.
And although the Pleasant Sunday Afternoon Society
now meets all week, although the slipper women
at the laundrette seem lively
and waves roll up in fits watching dunes
fail to outwit caravans,
it's a bad time.

We are alone together.
Even our jeweller's stopped twinkling.
You can't help but feel
someone out there might be planning chainsaw
psychiatry or florist pressing.

John Davies

***

Discussion

The phrase 'rural Wales' suggests peace as well as beauty. But what tensions have you found in the poems set there? Do you feel strongly about any of the issues raised?

*

In terms of what they're saying, is there any connection between Christine Evans' poem and Tony Connor's? (Both poets were born in England, incidentally.)

*

Once, says R.S. Thomas in his poem 'The Chapel', preachers 'caught fire/ and burned steadily' with belief. What makes people catch fire these days?

The Sea, The Sea

To live, as I did for eight years, on the estate of St Donat's Castle on the South Glamorgan coast, was to be everywhere in sight of the sea and — at first, anyway — everywhere to glimpse ideas for a novel. The Castle and grounds now form the campus of Atlantic College, where my wife taught English and,briefly, I too taught part-time. But formerly — in the Twenties and Thirties — they were the property of a man whose life has much to fascinate, if little to recommend, namely William Randolph Hearst.

Hearst was the American newspaper-owner, multimillionaire and megalomaniac on whom Orson Welles's great film *Citizen Kane* was based. Actually, St Donat's was only one of Hearst's *pieds-à-terre* in Europe; he had a *château* in France and a *schloss* in Germany too — not to mention his custom-built palace of San Simeon (the mausoleum-like 'Xanadu' of Kane) back home in California. In fact, Hearst seems almost to have collected castles, acquiring them as other rich Americans of his day might have built up a string of polo ponies. Given this, it's not surprising that the amount of time Hearst actually spent at St Donat's didn't add up to much. But tales are still told of how, occasionally in the summer months, contingents of glamorous house-guests — many of them famous Hollywood stars — would be whisked in limousines through the dumbfounded villages, on their way to the castle for a party which might last a leisurely fortnight or simply all weekend. They would dine in the great banqueting-hall, the magnificent coffered ceiling of which — like so much else in the castle and grounds — Hearst had imported intact from Italy. Afterwards they would stroll in the terraced formal gardens that successively led you down to the open air swimming pool and what was effectively a private beach. Or they might sit out of the wind in one of the several summerhouses — each equipped with a telephone, so that Hearst could be in touch with business interests elsewhere in the world. The outside phones have all been disconnected now, of course. Hearst is dead. So is his mistress and life's love Marion Davies, for whom he bought St Donat's as 'a present'. Many of the international students who now come to St Donat's will never have heard of either of them — nor even of the filmstars and other celebrities who came here once. The only hint of the castle's slightly scandalous, if intermittent, former glamour lies in the three unlikely and somewhat forlorn-looking palm trees that grow down in the valley, alongside the genuine 13th Century stone church: trees I liked to think Hearst had planted to remind him of California, and which I never passed without thinking of Hearst himself. Yes, there was certainly enough material and atmosphere for a novel in all this. And, who knows, if the novelist can avoid the twin traps of imitating Welles's Expressionist gloom and/or Scott Fitzgerald's tragic wistfulness, one day someone may even find it worth the writing.

But, for my own part, the novel — *Glass Shot* — which I finally started while I lived at St Donat's, and which was published shortly after we left that area, was more concerned with urban and rural landscapes elsewhere in South Wales. And, instead of monomanic and hubristic tycoons like Hearst or Kane or Gatsby, the main characters I have been dealing with, then and since, are a garage mechanic and an unemployed youth...But I note that a scene in *Glass Shot* is set at Sully Island, just along the coast from St Donats's — and that another, in the new novel I'm working on now, is set on a beach some way to the west...None of the characters in these novels is myself. But I know that my coming back to this particular area was important — as if, in order to unlock certain possibilities as a writer, I had to come back to this coastline, these particular stretches of cliffs, and beaches, and sea...For, to speak in terms of the 'writer's imagination' — that dialogue between self and circumstance — it was the sight and presence of the sea which were more resonant to me than that seductive but slightly snobbish nostalgia implicit in thoughts of the fabulously wealthy people who once happened to spend a little time upon this coast.

For me the sea's importance derives from memories of this entire coastline, which date from when I was a child. In fact, for a long period when I lived in other places, it was always a certain stretch of the South Glamorgan coast that I thought of in the occasional bouts of homesickness I indulged in in Kenilworth, or Leamington Spa, or Durham (North Carolina), or Manchester, or Oxford, or Tilbury, or Gravesend — residence in ten different towns or cities in as many years, I calculated once. But every person living away from home has not only a particular region he or she feels separated from but a very specific, intimately-known corner of it. It's not, finally, a country or even a particular town or city that you dream of returning to, but a single street or a unique horizon of hills. I was born in Cardiff, and grew up in the northern suburbs; but the place I felt closest to was the coast to the west of the city and, in particular, Lavernock: that muddy, sometimes smelly beach a mile down the coast, and a long way down-market, from Penarth: the beach that Cardiff people used to go on those summer Sundays of my boyhood — for an exile dreams, after all, of returning not only to the mythic landscape, but in vague quest for some former self, a golden age. Lavernock was not only a place I used to go to, it was a paradigmatic experience in time; it was a crystallisation of the always-irrecoverable past.

It was those early Sunday mornings in summer, still cool before the heat, and a press of families standing on the platform at Llandaff North station waiting for a train that was already half full, and that would be packed to standing-room only by the time it left Grangetown, two stops later. It was the 'Yankee comic' I had been bought at the newsagents' for the journey — a 'Lash LaRue' perhaps, or a 'Pecos Bill'. Then, when the train finally reached the little station at Lavernock — two platforms and a cream picket fence at the edge of a hayfield — it was the halfmile walk down that country lane between the fields to reach the beach, the crowd now strung out, as on a pilgrimage.

This was the middle Fifties: the halcyon days before diesel trains, before Beeching. They were compartment trains, without corridors, and the seats had a dusty reek never encountered since. Above were luggage racks of netted cord, like hammocks, and a foxed mirror between those sempiternally sunny monochromes of Great Yarmouth or the Wye at Symonds Yat. To lower the window you tugged, and released, a leather belt like a razor strop; and when you thrust out your abruptly windblown head — one of many infant heads along your side of the swaying train — you had to keep your eyes screwed up when looking front in case of specks of hot coal in the warm, blustery slipstream buffeting your face.

This was also a time when few members of the working class owned cars, which meant that other places on the coast — Llantwit Major or Ogmore or St Donat's itself — were out of reach. The trains didn't go there, and it was too far to cycle. You might get to Llantwit or Ogmore once a year, on the back of the lorry in the 'Whitsun Treat'. But otherwise — if you lived in Cardiff, at least — you went unfailingly to Lavernock. People 'from the Valleys' (i.e. anywhere north of Tongwynlais) were rumoured to prefer Barry Island, however: overcrowded, crass, commercialised, expensive Barry. The reasons for this were unknown, but had, presumably, to do with that general cultural benightedness and gullibility attributed by all city-dwellers to those who live in the hinterland. (Actually, it was probably a matter of which local rail line you were on for the coast.)

Lavernock, in any case, was much more basic. True, there was the nautically-named 'Golden Hind', a members-only drinking club. But apart from this, when you came off the country road, it was just a dust-and-gravel pathway down among the trees, the exposed roots of which were shiny from decades of footsoles. Then there were a couple of white-painted wooden shacks; these were boarded up and empty for seven or eight months of the year, but in the summer they

sold the usual necessities: icecreams, tin buckets and spades, rainbow-whorled rubber balls, pink candyfloss, more Yankee comics, sandwiches and teas (with large deposit against return of teapot, cups, spoon, try, etc.). There were also a pair of vile, fly-murmurous 'toilets' — latrine-sheds that led, it was believed, directly into the rusty, half-buried sewage pipe that ran a little way down from the upper part of the beach before disappearing into the sand, only to debouch, presumably, somewhere out in the Channel. I — in any case, and I assume, most people — rarely used this amenity. We would simply wade out for another swim instead, on the cynical, urban assumption that it would all end up there anyway.

When the tide was right out the beach, on the right-hand side, was a promontory of seaweed and grey mud, then rocks and rock pools. In the middle, far out, were rippled sandbanks and marooned lagoons. Higher up, though, there was usually a sufficient area of flat, hard sand to permit the bare-chested football game that seemed always to be in progress and that, as an onlooker, I remember as always involving full teams, a nearly full-sized pitch, an almost professional degree of sweat and combativeness and, in fact, one or two players who were 'on the City's books'. These games seemed to cease only when the tide was right in, whereupon the beach became suddenly almost as packed as the succession of trains which had supplied it. This was the time to take out the last few tomato sandwiches — which had become compressed in the bag — and the second flask of tea. Even the kids and the tireless, obsessive football-players would be forced either to go in for a swim or, finally, sit with everyone else on the narrow strip of rocks and round grey pebbles at the foot of the cliffs, watching the sunlit brown waves rise and break a few yards from your feet. Later on in the Fifties, my family acquired its own transport — a green van — and we began to go further along the coast on these Sunday outings: to Llantwit, mostly. But for some reason I began to feel more out of things on these trips. I suppose I was the forerunner of someone I later wrote a poem about:

A morose
solitary child, too old for his parents,
slumps in the back seat at a lay-by, watches
the cars blur past...

It wasn't just a question of my age. Places like Llantwit and Ogmore always had a faintly genteel air, one of Morris estate cars and primuses and tablecloths spread on the grass; and everybody parked, and sat, as far as possible from everybody else. What I missed was the proletarian populousness, or intimacy, or coarseness, or whatever it was, of Lavernock. And it occurs to me only now that those born after the Fifties in Cardiff will probably never realise how important 'going down the bay' was in the city's culture: part of a simultaneously marine and urban culture that has always seemed to me as profanely physical and open air as that of Camus' Oran, as tough and streetwise as that of Pasolini's Rome.

Of course, that Lavernock is gone now. Trains no longer stop at the little station, and the fields at the top of the cliff above the beach are now a caravan park. And, since whoever owns these fields also owns access — or at least parking — this beach too has now effectively been privatised. Ironically, I suppose, many of the caravans seem to be owned by Cardiffians of about my own age who, doubtless, once came there as kids, on the train from Llandaff North or Cardiff General or Grangetown, just as I did. Do they, too, miss the old Lavernock? I doubt it. In some ways — at least financially — they are better off than their parents were in the Fifties. They have the cars and the caravans their parents didn't, and why not? Probably it was only living away that made the place, and that period, so important in my memory. There is, after all, in some a nostalgia for the demotic just as surely as there is, in others, for the aristocratic.

Anyway, when my wife and first son and I came back to South Wales, to St Donat's, in the summer of 1982, I saw that what *was* still here, what hadn't changed, was the coastline and the cliffs, and not just at Lavernock but all along that familiar wavering bulge just west of the inlet that is Cardiff on the map: those eroding grey-and-yellow limestone cliffs barred horizontally with strata, like the breast of the honey-buzzard in the birdbook. I was thirtyfive years old — half the biblical span; and I felt it had taken all of that for those cliffs to show through in me, as a rock formation wears through topsoil.

And of course there was the sea itself. The sea has always been important to the imaginative life of South Walians: not only because of a maritime past, and the stories which came out of that, but because of ordinary but ineradicable private memories, like those I'm writing about here, and which all littoral peoples share. Perhaps this sense is best expressed by the exultant massed shout of *'Thalassa! Thalassa!'* in Xenophon when, after weeks of travelling, the sea is finally descried; and any kid who has ever been to Lavernock or Barry or Porthcawl on a summer daytrip will have experienced that moment too. Here, of course, it is no wine-dark Aegean that we confront but, often enough, that cement-grey gleam of the Bristol Channel under a wash of low cloud. But that instant of simultaneous expectedness and surprise, that slight lift to the heart, remains the same; and I experienced it undiminished — almost every day, I suppose — for those eight years at St Donat's when, at certain points of the road or turns in the driveways, suddenly the sea, and on a clear day Devon, were glimpsed across the last fields.

This has been a slightly roundabout narrative; but then, so was the biography which brought me back. These things are difficult enough to speak of; the working of landscape on our deepest imaginative life, on the daily emotion of living, is, like that of the weather, profound but inexpressible. But I've been aware that my personal history is again bound up with this coastline where I lived. It was not only the sense of place but the experience of coming back which influenced my work in some way, I would guess — though these things are mysterious — and perhaps by giving it not so much specific location as a simple rootedness, and for the first time in many years. Perhaps writing, like electricity, sometimes needs to be earthed.

Not that there is any guarantee that this will be enough even to light the single sixty-watt lightbulb in that naked, urban room that must also be part of the imaginative terrain of anyone writing in our time and which, no matter where we may have started out from, all of us — you, me, William Randolph Hearst, Charles Foster Kane, Jay Gatsby, F. Scott Fitzgerald, and whoever 'Rosebud' was — are terrified of ending up in.

Duncan Bush

Welsh History

We were a people taut for war; the hills
Were no harder, the thin grass
Clothed them more warmly than the coarse
Shirts our small bones.
We fought, and were always in retreat,
Like snow thawing upon the slopes
Of Mynydd Mawr; and yet the stranger
Never found our ultimate stand
In the thick woods, declaiming verse
To the sharp prompting of the harp.

Our kings died, or they were slain
By the old treachery at the ford.
Our bards perished, driven from the halls
Of nobles by the thorn and bramble.

We were a people bred on legends,
Warming our hands at the red past.
The great were ashamed of our loose rags
Clinging stubbornly to the proud tree
Of blood and birth, our lean bellies
And mud houses were a proof
Of our ineptitude for life.

We were a people wasting ourselves
In fruitless battles for our masters,
In lands to which we had no claim,
With men for whom we felt no hatred.

We were a people, and are so yet.
When we have finished quarrelling for crumbs
Under the table, or gnawing the bones
Of a dead culture, we will arise,
Armed, but not in the old way.

R.S. Thomas

Suggestions

Oral

Which poems of place have meant most to you? (Which covered the most familiar territory? Which most made you want to visit a particular place — or definitely not visit?)

Referring to his upbringing in 'the place I happened to be,' a character in one of R.S. Thomas' poems (not in this book) says: 'All right I was Welsh. Does it matter? ' Does that sum-up your feeling about the place — town, area, country — in which you've been brought up?

Writing

In his poem 'Synopsis of the Great Welsh Novel', Harri Webb imagines a novel set in an industrial valley. Write a story in which a film crew arrives to make a film in your area.

You've read John L. Hughes' and Duncan Bush's responses to their places, writers very different but alike in mixing information, opinion and imagination. What is it like where you live? (Write this as a letter, if you wish.)

'Where you live is who you are.' To what extent is this true, in your opinion?

Write a descriptive piece in response to one or both of the photographs in this section.

Poetry

'No one can write or even enjoy poetry,' wrote Lord Macauley, 'without a certain unsoundness of mind.' In writing a poem, try approaching your subject, your chosen place, from odd angles. Say you're writing about the sea: what is the sea talking about? How does it feel after a hard day's work ? A ship on the horizon is like... What kind of person is the lighthouse? What do gulls know about the sea that we don't? Make notes, collect images, and sort them out later.

Your place writes a poem about you.

Remember 'Swonzee Boy See'? Could you write a poem about your area in its own voice? That's difficult... It's hard to hear ourselves. What about a poem in the style of 'What Can You Give Me?' and using place names from your area? (The poem could be cheerful rather than a lament.)

Literature

(Focus on about three poems in responding to the subject of your choice, and don't forget to quote.)

Write on one of the subjects raised under 'Discussion' earlier, or under 'Oral' above.

Outline your point of view in response to one of these statements:

a) There is not just one Wales.

b) The past lives on in the present.

c) The main interest of any place lies in its individual lives.

Contrast one poem about rural Wales with one about urban Wales.

Relationships

Words in Focus

To relate a story is to tell it. The word 'relate' (or 'relation') is a link between the art of short story-writing and the relationships between people. Most of what we feel for and about each other is unspoken. Partly this is because no relationship could survive total honesty, with every irritation dragged wriggling to the surface. But it's also unspoken because, often, it's a mystery. We hardly understand ourselves let alone what's happening between us and other people.

And that's reflected in good fiction. A writer will, as does life itself, leave us room for discovery. There will be hints, suggestions... We make of them what we can. It's with the question of how we judge characters in fiction (based on what are, after all, only black marks on a white page) that this section of the book is concerned.

At its heart a relationship is like a triangle. Its three points are the writer, the words, the reader.

A Moonlight Gallop

Most weekends when the weather was good enough I used to go cycling in the mountains, usually the Brecon Beacons or the Black Mountains near the Herefordshire border. At that time, when I was about fifteen, I used to belong to the Youth Hostel Association, and so did Del Wellington and Charlie Bond, my friends. We used to pay a membership fee of five shillings a year and in return we got an enamel badge and a card to show we belonged to the Association; we were also sent a map which showed the location of all the Youth Hostels, most of them remote farmhouses, where we could stay for a night or two. Occasionally during the winter we'd plan, with the help of such a map, an immense journey through the dales of Yorkshire, unimaginably distant and foreign, knowing we'd never get there.

We knew all the hostels within possible cycling distance of our homes, although we rarely used them. Del's father had given us a heavy tent, already old, and we preferred to lug this about with us. We must have looked very odd on our three decrepit cycles — mine was rescued from the scrapyard and restored with loving care and some curious home-made fittings — all our strange equipment tied about us. Del always carried the tent on his bike, its bulk of canvas folded in an awkward sausage and slung beneath his cross-bar. It was so big that he had to ride bowlegged.

We had great times. Once we camped on a high moor in mid-Wales and I awoke in the middle of the night. I poked my head out of the tent into a moonlight whiter than frost, and all around us, still as wool, the sheep stood, hundreds of them, staring at the tent. I got back into my blankets and went to sleep and when the morning came there were no sheep to be seen anywhere. I didn't say a word about them to Del and Charlie.

I remember, too, camping near the foot of a waterfall. We hadn't meant to stay overnight, but we'd been attracted by the voice of the water, had pushed our bikes over a wet meadow towards the stream, and followed it up about four hundred yards until we reached the waterfall. It wasn't very high, perhaps sixty feet, but it was perfect. The white fall, never more than a foot wide, bent slowly over a ledge of rock and dropped without check into the pool beneath. We bathed in this pool. It was deep, cold enough to make us gasp, and the cleanest water I have ever used. It made our skins unrecognisable to us, as if a slippery layer of something had been stripped off us for the first time in our lives.

It took us quite a while to drag our gear up to the pool, and it wasn't easy to pitch our tent there, but we did it at last and went to sleep listening to the water's muted thunder. In the morning the green sun filtered down to us through the over-hanging branches of the trees overhead, and through the nodding ferns on the wet rocks. I could have stayed there forever.

That year we got away as often as we could. Perhaps it was a natural restlessness, the wish to see over the next hill, and the next; perhaps we realised that time was already beginning to run out for us, that there were responsibilities we would have to recognise, as well as the attractions of more sophisticated and less perfect pleasures. Whatever it was, hardly a week went by without us moving north into the deep mountains, slowly through the little villages climbing the one road out, merrily over the bare uplands guarded by buzzards. After a while we ventured farther afield; leaving our tent behind and using the Youth Hostels.

Towards the end of July the weather turned unseasonably bad. There was heavy rain, and a brutal wind sprang up in the evenings. The last Friday was depressing and we decided at school that we could go nowhere that weekend. I got home about five and began to read, eating some food aimlessly and without savour. The doorbell rang and my mother answered it. After a little while Charlie Bond came in. He had his cycle cape over his shoulders. It was black, with a hood.

'What do you think?' said Charlie.

I looked out of the window. The rain had stopped and a faint, watery sun showed tentatively behind the clouds.

'I don't know,' I said.

'It'll be good,' said Charlie. 'The wind's dropped and it's cool enough for a fast ride. Del's coming.'

'Mrs Wellington is never going to let Del go out in this weather!' said my mother. 'There must be something wrong with her! Well, you're not going, my boy, so don't ask it.'

The way she spoke I knew it was all right, so I grinned at her and got ready. I pushed my bike outside — Charlie's was leaning against the kerb.

'Where's Del?' I said.

'I haven't been over yet,' said Charlie. 'I only said he was coming so that it would be easier to persuade your mother.'

Together we called for Del and I suppose we were on our way before six o'clock. Everything went right for us. Before we were out of town the sun was shining and the evening had miraculously cleared. Without our tent we went at a fast clip, and there seemed about us all a surplus of energy which we controlled and directed into the expert handling of our cycles. We were over the crest of the mountain and dropping down into Abergavenny by seven. I can't remember that we ever had a better ride, the roads clear and kind, and we knowing each other so well that there was no need for talking.

Del had the maps, and he led us out on the Hereford road for a few miles before turning left onto a narrow lane. The light was still good and the sky unclouded above the valley along which we rode. I've never been in so still a place. Although we passed a few cottages at the side of the road, we saw nobody. It was as if the whole valley were deserted, its windows blind to our passing.

We began to climb, very gently at first, and the hollow valley opened out a little. The hedges were smaller and scrubbier and we could see over them into the fields they protected. As we climbed we could see, a long way off, the ruins of an abbey, its solid wall so pierced by the procession of great arched windows through which we saw the lit hills behind that it appeared insubstantial, a tracery of stone. The long evening sun shone fully upon it, on the tall decay of its towers, on its useless pillars. When at last we reached it, we found it standing back off the road, about two hundred yards back. We went in and wandered about for a bit, leaving our bikes leaning against the hedge. Charlie Bond, his hands hidden in his cycle cape, the black hood on his head, stepped mournfully through the cloisters, intoning as he went. He was a brilliant mimic, was Charlie. He could sing so exactly like Bing Crosby that Eustace Berry, a boy in our class, used to come miles out of his way just to walk to school with Charlie, listening to him sing. Now Charlie trod softly on the grass between the fallen walls, his face hidden under his cowl, his echoing, faulty Latin moving and ominous. It was amusing too, but I was glad when Del said, 'Stow it, Charlie. We've still got a fair way to go.'

And at once I became aware of the fading light. Back down the valley there was a hint of twilight about the farms and the tall trees, and a soft mist was beginning to fill the fields near the river.

'That's for heat,' said Charlie. 'Positively it will be very hot tomorrow.'

'I worry about tonight,' Del said: 'We have to be in the hostel by nine, and then we have our supper to cook. I'm starving.'

We had a look at the large-scale map. We had at least five miles to go and up hills so steep that the contour lines pressed hard against each other.

'Look at those lines,' said Charlie. 'They'd depress an active goat.'

We swung our legs over our saddles and rode on. Pretty soon, so steep had the climb become, we were forced to dismount and push the bikes. The fields had given way to harsh moorland, cropped by ponies. Here and there the heather and poor grass were broken by

stony outcrops. Nothing moved at all. The long shadows merged imperceptibly into a continuous darkness.

'We'll be late,' Del said.

'If we find it,' said Charlie.

Del only grunted. This was a hostel we had never visited, but we had seen it often enough on the map. We knew exactly where it was. We pushed on, searching the moor for a light. The moon came up, brilliantly lucid, and we felt more cheerful, singing gently together.

It was Del who saw the light, high on our left hand, and he led us without a falter along the rough path which led to the house. We were all glad to get there and laughed and joked as we knocked on the door. It was nearly ten o'clock.

Mrs Devereux let us in. She was the warden's wife, a tall, unfriendly woman. When she spoke, her voice was slow and surprisingly soft and she spoke with a Midlands accent. I thought she might have come from Birmingham. Her husband stood silently in the kitchen. They were not welcoming.

'You boys are late,' he said.

'I know,' I answered. 'We're sorry. We didn't know the climb would be so steep — we thought we had plenty of time.'

'You know the rules,' he said, 'I'd be within my rights to turn you away.'

We stood there, not answering.

'They might as well stay, Jack,' said Mrs Devereux, timidly. 'There's nobody else here. They look tired.'

He didn't answer so I took his silence for agreement.

'We'll bring the bikes in,' I said.

He looked at me for the first time, leaning, his hands flat on the kitchen table. He was a stocky man, his broad shoulders filling the flannel shirt he wore, but his face was worn tight down almost to the bone and his eyes were set deep. There was no expression at all on his face, unless it was a kind of impersonal weariness.

We went outside to bring in the cycles.

'Leave them in the passage,' said Mr Devereux as we went.

Outside, in the light of the one electric bulb set high in the wall,

I looked at Del and Charlie. They looked quiet and withdrawn, and they did not meet my gaze.

'Cheer up, boys,' I said.

'You must be mad,' said Del, 'but speak to me after supper.'

When we got back in I asked Mr Devereux where we could cook our supper.

'There'll be no cooking here,' he said.

'But we've had nothing to eat for hours,' I protested, indignation making my voice sharp. 'You can let us heat a can of beans, at least!'

Del and Charlie stood behind me, saying nothing, leaving it to me. Mr Devereux looked from one to the other of us, his dead face empty. He waved a hand briefly.

'The wife will give you a mug of cocoa,' he said, 'and if you have bread and cheese you can eat that.'

We settled for that, sitting around the scrubbed table. The cocoa was scaldingly hot and sweet and we drank it without a word. Devereux and his wife sat each side of the fireplace, on long settles. There was an unbelievably tense air about them and they never stopped watching us. The second that Charlie finished his food, Devereux stood up.

'Come on,' he said, 'I'll show you the dormitory.'

We collected our sleeping bags and our rucksacks and followed him out of the back door. We were in a courtyard perhaps fifty yards square, cobbled and empty. The house itself formed one side of the square, and long farm buildings the other three sides. At the far end was the stable-block, two-storied like the house, and this is where he took us. We climbed up the open wooden stairs and into the long room. It was immaculately swept and clean, its short walls white-washed with lime, the windows uncurtained. There was no light, but the clear moon streamed in and we could see easily.

'Here you are,' said Mr Devereaux, his whole manner suddenly more relaxed and friendly. 'You'll be comfortable here. Get off to sleep as soon as you can.'

We heard him go down the stairs and pull the door behind him. The latch fell with a smooth click. Charlie Bond began to giggle.

'You certainly told him,' he said to me. 'You should have seen your face when you thought you weren't going to have any supper!'

'Why not?' said Del. 'You'd have grumbled most if we had come to bed with empty stomachs.'

There were hand basins at the far end of the room and we washed in the cold water, unrolled our sleeping bags and threw them on three beds near one of the windows. We turned in fairly soon. Normally we would have talked together for an hour, but we didn't say much that night and everything grew still. I don't know whether

Charlie and Del slept, but I certainly didn't. I was happy and warm there, and I began to think of Charlie walking down the darkening cloisters of the abbey, his voice echoing along the roofless walls. I saw once again the regular turning of Del's legs and feet as he pedalled along in front of me on the road to Abergavenny, monotonously around and around. I expect I was going to sleep.

What brought me to my feet was startling enough. A door opened in the courtyard, then there was a confused clatter of feet. That was all right. It was the scream that stretched me. Not a scream of fright, but a high-pitched, whinnying scream, rather like that of a horse. And then there was a regular, light, galloping sound on the cobbles below. I was at the window at once, Del and Charlie looking over my shoulders.

The moonlight had divided the courtyard into almost exact halves, the area near us being brilliantly lit, that against the house in deep shadow. Mr and Mrs Devereux stood in the full moonlight, close together, almost in the centre of the yard. Mr Devereux had a rope in his hands. It reached into the shadow, and Mr Devereux and his wife turned slowly, facing the galloping as it raced through the darkness. We did not know what to expect.

Out into the moonlight, roped about his waist, raced a boy of our own age, his arms thrashing the air, his unkempt pale hair bouncing on his head. Round and round he went, his heavy boots thumping and sparking on the cobbles, in and out of the revealing light. His face as he raced towards us was empty, an idiot's face; froth was forming around his mouth. Every time he raced into the dark, he screamed his shaken cry.

After a while, Devereux pulled in the rope, taking the boy in his arms. Now that he was still, we could see that the boy was unbelievably bent and frail. He could not walk properly, but that may have been from exhaustion. They went, all three, into the house, closing the door so softly that we could not hear it at all.

Del and Charlie were sitting on their beds, their faces turned towards the window, appalled and horrified. I don't know what we said to each other, or indeed if we said anything at all at that time.

That was thirty years ago. On holiday last year, driving aimlessly in the region, I came across the valley once again. I didn't recognise it at first. The road was wider and better surfaced, and there was an air of prosperity about the place. But the abbey was the same. There were many visitors there, and I walked along the grass, remembering Charlie Bond who was killed in Africa in 1942 and Del Wellington who lives somewhere near Manchester and is a chemist.

I drove on, up the hill. The Youth Hostel is still there, still a hostel. It was a warm day, full of summer, but momentarily all I saw were the lucid moonlight and the faces of my two friends, as clear as my hand; all I heard was a ragged galloping over the cobbles.

Leslie Norris

***

Discussion

Straight away the narrator in 'A Moonlight Gallop' presents us with a relationship, 'I' becoming 'we'. As he cycles with Del and Charlie through an almost dream country, the innocence of their travelling is suggested: the roads are 'clear and kind' and they find 'the cleanest water I have ever used'. Then the word 'responsibilities' lands like a boulder on the road. 'Perhaps we realized that time was already beginning to run out for us, that there were responsibilities we would have to recognise.' What does the word suggest to you?

Leslie Norris enriches his meaning by connections which give it a nudge. As the narrator falls asleep at the hostel, for instance, he's thinking contentedly of the day's cycling. Then he is woken by a scream, sees a boy his own age also locked in effort, and the connection makes the boy's 'thrashing the air' seem all the more desperate. Such links can be made between what people say or do not say as well as between their actions. The narrator's mother firmly rejects his request to go cycling but 'the way she spoke I knew it was alright'. Later in the story, 'Mr. Devereux didn't answer so I took his silence for agreement'. Adults often take shelter cautiously, the writer suggests, in mock refusal or silence. The part that silence can play in relationships clearly interests him. The boys know 'each other so well that there was no need for talking' about the experiences they share. But what about the ones they don't ? When the narrator sees something haunting, hundreds of sheep staring at him in moonlight, 'I didn't say a word about them to Del and Charlie'. Why not, do you think?

*

A good writer might also try to present, in the interests of truth, more than just one point of view. To the boys, Mrs Devereux is a 'tall, unfriendly woman'. She and her husband 'were not welcoming'; he looked at the boys, 'his dead face empty'. And yet. Is there evidence that Mrs Devereux is not really unkind?

And (especially since we know the end of the story) what might make us sympathetic in this description of her husband: 'He was a stocky man, his broad shoulders filling the flannel shirt he wore, but his face was worn tight down almost to the bone and his eyes were set deep. There was no expression at all on his face, unless it was a kind of impersonal weariness'?

People, the writer indicates, are not simple. Although Mrs Devereux is 'unwelcoming', her voice is 'soft'. The stern Mr Devereux is also 'Jack'. We are encouraged to open ourseves to more than one point of view, one version of the truth. When he shows the boys to their dormitory, Mr Devereux says in an almost fatherly way, 'You'll be comfortable here'. And what we first assume to be some kind of torture of the son ('he screamed his shaken cry') turns out to be — what?

*

Finally, there is the power of imagery to convey meanings which plain statement might make too simple or crude. Take the image of moonlight: 'Round and round he went, his heavy boots thumping and sparking on the cobbles, in and out of the revealing light'. On one level, it is the light of the moon, revealing a boy plunging around in a circle. But what, in a more general sense, is revealed to these healthy boys who had set out on a contented journey?

What the moonlight reveals here is a long way from what it revealed in the third paragraph: placid white sheep. It is partly from what's unexplained, from contrasts and images and different points of view, that good writing draws its power.

Voices

Patricia, Edith, and Arnold

The small boy in his invisible engine, the Cwmdonkin Special, its wheels, polished to dazzle, crunching on the small back garden scattered with breadcrumbs for the birds and white with yesterday's snow, its smoke rising thin and pale as breath in the cold afternoon, hooted under the wash-line, kicked the dog's plate at the washhouse stop, and puffed and pistoned slower and slower while the servant girl lowered the pole, unpegged the swinging vests, showed the brown stains under her arms, and called over the wall; 'Edith, Edith, come here, I want you.'

Edith climbed on two tubs on the other side of the wall and called back: 'I'm here, Patricia.' Her head bobbed up above the broken glass.

He backed the Flying Welshman from the washhouse to the open door of the coal-hole and pulled hard on the brake that was a hammer in his pocket: assistants in uniform ran out with fuel; he spoke to a saluting fireman, and the engine shuffled off, round the barbed walls of China that kept the cats away, by the frozen rivers in the sink, in and out of the coal-hole tunnel. But he was listening carefully all the time, through the squeals and whistles, to Patricia and the next-door servant, who belonged to Mrs Lewis, talking when they should have been working, calling his mother Mrs T., being rude about Mrs L.

He heard Patricia say: 'Mrs T. won't be back till six.'

And Edith next door replied: 'Old Mrs L. has gone to Neath to look for Mr Robert.'

'He's on the randy again,' Patricia whispered.

'Randy, sandy, bandy!' cried the boy out of the coal-hole.

'You get your face dirty, I'll kill you,' Patricia said absent-mindedly.

She did not try to stop him when he climbed up the coal-heap. He stood quietly on the top, King of the Coal Castle, his head touching the roof, and listened to the worried voices of the girls. Patricia was almost in tears, Edith was sobbing and rocking on the unsteady tubs. 'I'm standing on top of the coal,' he said, and waited for Patricia's anger.

She said: 'I don't want to see him, you go alone.'

'We must, we must go together,' said Edith. 'I've got to know.'

'I don't want to know.'

'I can't stand it, Patricia, you must go with me.'

'You go alone, he's waiting for you.'

'Please, Patricia!'

'I'm lying on my face in the coal,' said the boy.

'No, it's your day with him. I don't want to know. I just want to think he loves me.'

'Oh, talk sense, Patricia, please! Will you come or no? I've got to hear what he says.'

'All right then, in half an hour. I'll shout over the wall.'

'You'd better come soon,' the boy said, 'I'm dirty as Christ knows what.'

Patricia ran to the coal-hole. 'The language! Come out of there at once!' she said.

The tubs began to slide and Edith vanished.

'Don't you dare use language like that again. Oh! Your suit!' Patricia took him indoors.

She made him change his suit in front of her. 'Otherwise there's no telling.' He took off his trousers and danced around her, crying: 'Look at me, Patricia!'

'You be decent,' she said, 'or I won't take you to the park.'

'Am I going to the park, then?'

'Yes, we're all going to the park; you and me and Edith next door.'

He dressed himself neatly, not to annoy her, and spat on his hands before parting his hair. She appeared not to notice his silence and neatness. Her large hands were clasped together; she stared down at the white brooch on her chest. She was a tall, thick girl with awkward hands, her fingers were like toes, her shoulders were wide as a man's.

'Am I satisfactory?' he asked.

'There's a long word,' she said, and looked at him lovingly. She lifted him up and seated him on the top of the chest of drawers. 'Now you're as tall as I am.'

'But I'm not so old,' he said.

He knew that this was an afternoon on which anything might happen; it might snow enough for sliding on a tray; uncles from America, where he had no uncles, might arrive with revolvers and St. Bernards; Ferguson's shop might catch on fire and all the piece-packets fall on the pavements; and he was not surprised when she put her black, straight-haired heavy head on his shoulder and whispered into his collar: 'Arnold, Arnold Matthews.'

'There, there,' he said, and rubbed her parting with his finger and winked at himself in the mirror behind her and looked down her dress at the back.

'Are you crying?'

'No.'

'Yes you are, I can feel the wet.'

She dried her eyes on her sleeve. 'Don't you let on that I was crying.'

'I'll tell everybody, I'll tell Mrs T. and Mrs L., I'll tell the policeman and Edith and my dad and Mr. Chapman, Patricia was crying on my shoulder like a nanny goat, she cried for two hours, she cried enough to fill a kettle. I won't really,' he said.

As soon as he and Patricia and Edith set off for the park, it began to snow. Big flakes unexpectedly fell on the rocky hill, and the sky grew dark as dusk though it was only three in the afternoon. Another boy, somewhere in the allotments behind the houses, shouted as the first flakes fell. Mrs Ocky Evans opened the top bay-windows of Springmead and thrust her head and hands out, as though to catch the snow. He waited, without revolt, for Patricia to say, 'Quick! hurry back, it's snowing!' and to pack him in out of the day before his feet were wet. Patricia can't have seen the snow, he thought at the top of the hill, though it was falling heavily, sweeping against her face, covering her black hat. He dared not speak for fear of waking her, as they turned the corner into the road that led down to the park. He lagged behind to take his cap off and catch the snow in his mouth.

'Put on your cap,' said Patricia, turning, 'Do you want to catch your death of cold?'

She tucked his muffler inside his coat, and said to Edith: 'Will he be there in the snow, do you think? He's bound to be there, isn't he? He was always there on my Wednesdays, wet or fine.'

The tip of her nose was red, her cheeks glowed like coals, she looked handsomer in the snow than in the summer, when her hair would lie limp on her wet forehead and a warm patch spread on her back.

'He'll be there,' Edith said. 'One Friday it was pelting down and he was there. He hasn't got anywhere else to go, he's always there. Poor Arnold!' She looked white and tidy in a coat with a fur piece, and twice as small as Patricia; she stepped through the thick snow as though she were going shopping.

'Wonders will never cease,' he said aloud to himself. This was Patricia letting him walk in the snow, this was striding along in a storm with two big girls. He sat down in the road. 'I'm on a sledge,' he said, 'pull me, Patricia, pull me like an Eskimo.'

'Up you get, you moochin, or I'll take you home.'

He saw that she did not mean it. 'Lovely Patricia, beautiful Patricia,' he said, 'pull me along on my bottom.'

'Any more dirty words, and you know who I'll tell.'

'Arnold Matthews,' he said.

Patricia and Edith drew closer together.

'He notices everything,' Patricia whispered.

Edith said: 'I'm glad I haven't got your job.'

'Oh,' said Patricia, catching him by the hand and pressing it on her arm, 'I wouldn't change him for the world!'

He ran down the gravel path on to the upper walk of the park.

'I'm spoilt!' he shouted, 'I'm spoilt! Patricia spoils me!'

Soon the park would be white all over; already the trees were blurred round the reservoir and fountain, and the training college on the gorse hill was hidden in a cloud. Patricia and Edith took the steep path down to the shelter. Following on the forbidden grass, he slid past them straight into a bare bush, but the bump and the pricks left him shouting and unhurt. The girls gossiped sadly now. They shook their coats in the deserted shelter, scattering snow on the seats, and sat down, close together still, outside the bowling-club window.

'We're only just on time,' said Edith. 'It's hard to be punctual in the snow.'

'Can I play by here?'

Patricia nodded. 'Play quietly then; don't be rough with the snow.'

'Snow! snow! snow!' he said, and scooped it out of the gutter and made a small ball.

'Perhaps he's found a job,' Patricia said.

'Not Arnold.'

'What if he doesn't come at all?'

'He's bound to come, Patricia; don't say things like that.'

'Have you brought your letters?'

'They're in my bag. How many have you got?'

'No, how many have you got, Edith?'

'I haven't counted.'

'Show me one of yours,' Patricia said.

He was used to their talk by this time; they were old and cuckoo, sitting in the empty shelter sobbing over nothing. Patricia was reading a letter and moving her lips.

'He told me that, too,' she said, 'that I was his star.'

'Did he begin: "Dear Heart"?'

'Always: "Dear Heart."'

Edith broke into real loud tears. With a snowball in his hand, he watched her sway on the seat and hide her face in Patricia's snowy coat.

Patricia said, patting and calming Edith, rocking her head: 'I'll give him a piece of my mind when he comes.'

When who comes? He threw the snowball high into the silently

driving fall. Edith's crying in the deadened park was clear and thin as a whistle, and, disowning the soft girls and standing away from them in case a stranger passed, a man with boots to his thighs, or a sneering, bigger boy from the Uplands, he piled the snow against the wire of the tennis court and thrust his hands into the snow like a baker making bread. As he delved and moulded the snow into loaves, saying under his breath, 'This is the way it is done, ladies and gentlemen,' Edith raised her head and said: 'Patricia, promise me, don't be cross with him. Let's all be quiet and friendly.'

'Writing, "Dear Heart" to us both,' said Patricia angrily. 'Did he ever take off your shoes and pull your toes and —'

'No, no, you mustn't, don't go on, you mustn't speak like that!' Edith put her fingers to her cheeks. 'Yes, he did,' she said.

'Somebody has been pulling Edith's toes,' he said to himself, and ran round the other side of the shelter, chuckling. 'Edith went to market,' he laughed aloud, and stopped at the sight of a young man without an overcoat sitting in the corner seat and cupping his hands and blowing into them. The young man wore a white muffler and a check cap. When he saw the boy, he pulled his cap down over his eyes. His hands were pale blue and the ends of his fingers yellow.

The boy ran back to Patricia. 'Patricia, there's a man!' he cried.

'Where's a man?'

'On the other side of the shelter; he hasn't got an overcoat and he's blowing in his hands like this.'

Edith jumped up. 'It's Arnold!'

'Arnold Matthews, Arnold Matthews, we know you're there!'

Patricia called round the shelter, and, after a long minute, the young man, raising his cap and smiling, appeared at the corner and leant against a wooden pillar.

The trousers of his sleek blue suit were wide at the bottoms; the shoulders were high and hard, and sharp at the ends; his pointed patent shoes were shining; a red handkerchief stuck from his breast pocket; he had not been out in the snow.

'Fancy you two knowing each other,' he said loudly, facing the red-eyed girls and motionless, open-mouthed boy who stood at Patricia's side with his pockets full of snowballs.

Patricia tossed her head and her hat fell over one eye. As she straightened her hat, 'You come and sit down here, Arnold Matthews, you've got some questions to answer!' she said in her washing-day voice.

Edith clutched at her arm: 'Oh! Patricia you promised.' She picked at the edge of her handkerchief. A tear rolled down her cheek.

Arnold said softly then: 'Tell the little boy to run away and play.'

The boy ran round the shelter once and returned to hear Edith saying: 'There's a hole in your elbow, Arnold,' and to see the young man kicking the snow at his feet and staring at the names and hearts cut on the wall behind the girls' heads.

'Who did you walk out with on Wednesdays?' Patricia asked. Her clumsy hands held Edith's letter close to the sprinkled folds of her chest.

'You, Patricia.'

'Who did you walk out with on Fridays?'

'With Edith, Patricia.'

He said to the boy: 'Here, son, can you roll a snowball as big as a football?'

'Yes, as big as two footballs.'

Arnold turned back to Edith, and said: 'How did you come to know Patricia Davies? You work in Brynmill.'

'I just started work in Cwmdonkin,' she said. 'I haven't seen you since, to tell you. I was going to tell you to-day, but I found out. How could you Arnold? Me on my afternoon off, and Patricia on Wednesdays.'

The snowball had turned into a short snow man with a lop-sided, dirty head and a face full of twigs, wearing a boy's cap and smoking a pencil.

'I didn't mean any harm,' said Arnold. 'I love you both.'

Edith screamed. The boy jumped forward and the snow man with a broken back collapsed.

'Don't tell your lies, how can you love two of us?' Edith cried, shaking her handbag at Arnold. The bag snapped open, and a bundle of letters fell on the snow.

'Don't you dare pick up those letters,' Patricia said.

Arnold had not moved. The boy was searching for his pencil in the snow man's ruins.

'You make your choice, Arnold Matthews, here and now.'

'Her or me,' said Edith.

Patricia turned her back to him. Edith, with her bag in her hand hanging open, stood still. The sweeping snow turned up the top page of a letter.

'You two,' he said, 'you go off the handle. Sit down and talk. Don't cry like that, Edith. Hundreds of men love more than one woman, you're always reading about it. Give us a chance, Edith, there's a girl.'

Patricia looked at the hearts and arrows and old names. Edith saw the letters curl.

'It's you, Patricia,' said Arnold.

Still Patricia stood turned away from him. Edith opened her mouth to cry, and he put a finger to his lips. He made the shape of a whisper, too soft for Patricia to hear. The boy watched him soothing and promising Edith, but she screamed again and ran out of the shelter and down the path, her handbag beating against her side.

'Patricia,' he said, 'turn round to me. I had to say it. It's you, Patricia.'

The boy bent down over the snow man and found his pencil driven through its head. When he stood up he saw Patricia and Arnold arm in arm.

Snow dripped through his pockets, snow melted in his shoes, snow trickled down his collar into his vest. 'Look at you now,' said Patricia, rushing to him and holding him by the hands, 'you're wringing wet.'

'Only a bit of snow,' said Arnold, suddenly alone in the shelter.

'A bit of snow indeed, he's as cold as ice and his feet are like sponges. Come on home at once!'

The three of them climbed the path to the upper walk, and Patricia's footprints were as large as a horse's in the thickening snow.

'Look, you can see our house, it's got a white roof!'

'We'll be there, ducky, soon.'

'I'd rather stay out and make a snow man like Arnold Matthews.'

'Hush! hush! your mother'll be waiting. You must come home.'

'No she won't. She gone on a randy with Mr Robert. Randy, sandy, bandy!'

'You know very well she's shopping with Mrs Partridge, you mustn't tell wicked lies.'

'Well Arnold Matthews told lies. He said he loved you better than Edith, and he whispered behind your back to her.'

'I swear I didn't, Patricia, I don't love Edith at all!'

Patricia stopped walking. 'You don't love Edith?'

'No, I've told you, it's you. I don't love her at all,' he said. 'Oh! my God, what a day! Don't you believe me? It's you Patricia. Edith isn't anything. I just used to meet her; I'm always in the park.'

'But you told her you loved her.'

The boy stood bewildered between them. Why was Patricia so angry and serious? Her face was flushed and her eyes shone. Her chest moved up and down. He saw the long black hairs on her leg through a tear in her stockings. Her leg is as big as my middle, he thought. I'm cold; I want tea; I've got snow in my fly.

Arnold backed slowly down the path. 'I had to tell her that or she wouldn't have gone away. I had to, Patricia. You saw what she was like. I hate her. Cross my heart!'

'Bang! bang!' cried the boy.

Patricia was smacking Arnold, tugging at his muffler, knocking him with her elbows. She pummelled him down the path, and shouted at the top of her voice: 'I'll teach you to lie to Edith! You pig! you black! I'll teach you to break her heart!'

He shielded his face from her blows as he staggered back. 'Patricia, Patricia, don't hit me! There's people!'

As Arnold fell, two women with umbrellas up peered through the whirling snow from behind a bush.

Patricia stood over him. 'You lied to her and you'd lie to me,' she said. 'Get up, Arnold Matthews!'

He rose and set his muffler straight and wiped his eyes with the red handkerchief, and raised his cap and walked toward the shelter.

'And as for you,' Patricia said, turning to the watching women, 'you should be ashamed of yourselves! Two old women playing about in the snow.'

They dodged behind the bush.

Patricia and the boy climbed, hand in hand, back to the upper walk.

'I've left my cap by the snow man,' he remembered. 'It's my cap with the Tottenham colours.'

'Run back quickly,' she said, 'you can't get any wetter than you are.'

He found his cap half hidden under snow. In a corner of the shelter, Arnold sat reading the letters that Edith had dropped, turning the wet pages slowly. He did not see the boy, and the boy, behind a pillar, did not interrupt him. Arnold read every letter carefully.

'You've been a long time finding your cap,' Patricia said. 'Did you see the young man?'

'No,' he said, 'he was gone.'

At home, in the warm living-room, Patricia made him change his clothes again. He held his hands in front of the fire, and soon they began to hurt.

'My hands are on fire,' he told her, 'and my toes, and my face.'

After she had comforted him, she said: 'There, that's better. The hurting's gone. You won't call the king your uncle in a minute.' She was bustling about the room. 'Now we've all had a good cry today.'

Dylan Thomas

***

Discussion

Two main points of view are presented at the same time in the story: the small boy's ('they were old and cuckoo, sitting in the empty shelter sobbing over nothing') and that of the girls. The girls see the snow, for instance, only as a nuisance. How does the boy see it? And what's the reason for this difference in point of view, do you think?

*

Dialogue should help carry the story forward or increase our knowledge in some way. How revealing do you find this part of the story?

> 'I'm standing on top of the coal,' he said, and waited for Patricia's anger.
>
> She said: 'I don't want to see him, you go alone.'
>
> 'We must, we must go together,' said Edith. 'I've got to know.'
>
> 'I don't want to know.'
>
> 'I can't stand it, Patricia, you must go with me.'
>
> 'You go alone, he's waiting for you.'
>
> 'Please, Patricia!'
>
> 'I'm lying on my face in the coal,' said the boy.
>
> 'No, it's your day with him. I don't want to know. I just want to think he loves me.'
>
> 'Oh, talk sense, Patricia, please! Will you come or no? I've got to hear what he says.'
>
> 'All right then, in half an hour. I'll shout over the wall.'
>
> 'You'd better come soon,' the boy said, 'I'm dirty as Christ knows what.'
>
> Patricia ran to the coal-hole. 'The language! Come out of there at once!' she said.

*

We meet Arnold Matthews only briefly but the writer has selected his details with care. What impression do you get of Arnold? You might consider these details amongst others:

'When he saw the boy, he pulled his cap down over his eyes.'

'Hundreds of men love more than one woman, you're always reading about it.'

'Patricia, don't hit me! There's people!'

*

Dylan Thomas is careful to present Patricia and Edith as individuals too, even though their point of view is broadly similar. In what way are they different? (Focus on precise details.)

*

How effective do you find Patricia's remark, 'Now we've all had a good cry today', as an ending to the story?

*

Without looking yet at the page from which it's taken, read the paragraph below then think of four words to include in the blanks.

> The small boy in his — engine, the Cwmdonkin Special, its wheels, polished to dazzle, crunching on the small back garden scattered with breadcrumbs for the birds and white with yesterday's snow, its smoke rising thin and pale as — in the cold afternoon, hooted under the wash-line, kicked the dog's plate at the washhouse stop, and puffed and — slower and slower while the servant girl lowered the pole, unpegged the — vests, showed the brown stains under her arms, and called over the wall; 'Edith, Edith, come here, I want you.'

Now check the story's first paragraph. Which word of yours, do you think, was most obviously as good as Dylan Thomas'? And which word of his was most obviously better than your choice? Why?

Pink Summer Blues

Last night I knew they knew. Just as soon as I saw Daz and his mob at the end of the street. They'd already seen me. If they hadn't, I could've sneaked down the path at the side of Snips and got home that way. Too late. I made myself walk tall and slow.

'Hey, look who it isn't.'

'It's that stuck up kid. Yer know, wot's 'er name.'

'Used to talk to us, didn't she? Thinks she's too good for us now. Stuck-up cow.'

I had to look at them, but with what sort of face? That stupid nerve in my cheek started twitching.

Daz was half sat, half slumped on the rail outside the chip shop. I concentrated inside and willed him not to get up on his feet. They'd take their cue from him. As long as he stayed relaxed, kind of casual like that, sneering but not really threatening, I might be O.K.

'Hafwen!' he shouted as I passed. Then straightaway he looked sideways at Gary. 'That her name, Gaz? It's something funny like that.'

'Yeah. Hafwen. Welsh, innit?'

'And what's her sister called?' I groaned deep down. So they knew alright.

'Leri, yeah?'

They were all laughing. Daz spoke very slowly, his voice heavy with mock concern. 'I've heard she's landed herself in a spot of bovver.'

'Something like that.'

He was looking straight at me. Dead sarcastic and cool. I didn't want to but I had to admire the way he handled it.

'You wouldn't believe, would you? I mean, they're such a *respectable* family.'

'But it's political, innit?'

'What's that, Gaz?'

'Well, second homes and protests. Welsh nationalists and that.'

'What's she done then?'

'Got into that new estate agent's in town and smashed the computers or something. Her and some of her mates. Then phoned the police to say they'd done it.'

'No.'

'Yeah.'

'She's in college, isn't she?'

'Yeah.'

'You'd think she'd know better, wouldn't you? I mean, educated and that.'

'Yeah, you would.'

They were enjoying this. Making a meal of it. Then the expression on Daz's face changed.

'You know what gets me about this, Gaz. Really pisses me off I mean, cos, you know how I hate injustice.' There was a buzz of relish all around.

'What's that?'

'If it was you and me did this, something like this, we'd get it wouldn't we? We'd go down. The works. We'd cop the lot. Breaking and entering. Criminal damage. She won't, you know.'

'How d'you reckon that?'

'Well, like you said, it's political. Different, isn't it?'

The words were out before I realised. 'It'll be treated just the same,' I said. 'She'll be charged just the same.' My face was burning, all the more as I realised I'd walked right into it. Just as he'd planned. 'She'll go to court and she'll probably go to prison. That's what she expects.'

'And wants? Wants to be a martyr? That's what it's all about, isn't it?' Then he looked away from me and back at his gang again. It was like he was conducting an orchestra. 'Hey listen, you lot. Did y'hear that? She can still talk when she wants to. She can still manage it. Didn't think you could, Hafwen. Thought you'd forgotten. How to speak English, I mean.'

I stared at him. My legs wanted to run, but the rest of me wanted to stay. Fight if necessary. But whose side was I on anyway? And it wasn't as if I even liked Leri half the time. And anyway Daz wasn't English. He wasn't proper Welsh either, not like my family, but you couldn't say he was English. And I was tired. My feet were aching. I felt sticky and the sweet stink of candy floss was stuck in my clothes, my hair. I could do without this. All of it.

Then, it was as if I was moving up on a sliding scale of anger, he said something that just finished me off.

'D'you know something, Gaz. She's not got bad legs, has she? Always got that bloody serious expression on her face, though. Puts you off.'

'Yeah,' said Gaz. 'Studious type.'

I wanted to hit them. Flatten them. But my anger just made me pathetic. They knew they'd got me riled and that inspired them all the more. Daz had a special line in sarcasm, and part of me, I had to admit, wanted to laugh. There'd been a poor supply of laughter in our house ever since Leri'd got into the language act and my mother was flopping round the house having nervous breakdowns all the time.

Now he was grinning all over his face.'If she's not careful she'll be going off to college like her sister and smashing computers too. D'you think there's a special course in it, Gaz? Can anyone get on it? What about us? I wouldn't mind a diploma in smashing computers, but they wouldn't call it that, would they?'

'No. They'd make it sound better than that. Something like computer demobilization...'

'Right. How about Computer Demobilization and Sabotage?'

I didn't know what to say. Or do. And I couldn't just creep away either. I was like a mesmerised rabbit. The rest of the gang was getting bored with it by now. They started shuffling their feet and a couple of them lit up. Little Andy Patterson started to blow smoke rings.

Sensing that this particular line of entertainment had run out of steam, Daz wound it up. He picked himself up from his perch and seemed to glide off with that peculiar drifting walk of his. The others just followed with hardly a backward glance, except for Gary, who looked as if there was more he wanted to say. It's weird, but left standing there I felt kind of lost. Was this the sort of kick Leri got out of her antics? I was just going to sidle off myself when Daz turned round and shouted, dead loud, so everyone on the estate could hear, 'When's it coming up in court, then?'

'I don't know,' I mumbled, ashamed of my feeble-sounding voice.

'I want to be kept informed,' he said, nudging Gary. 'I want to be kept up to date with the latest developments.'

And at last I managed to show a bit of life. 'Of course,' I said, as if I'd been a student at Daz's very own school of street cred. 'I'll make certain you get regular bulletins. Watch this space.'

And when they'd disappeared round the corner at last, the street looked so dull and dead.

*

I know I moan and groan about this job but I like it really. I like the whirr and hum the drum makes as it turns. Pouring the hard shiny crystals of sugar into the funnel thing in the middle is good too. I can't explain why, but there's something really satisfying about measuring out those shocking pink grains. Perhaps it's the way they glitter. Like rubies, I don't know. And I love the look on the kids' faces. It's a kind of magic to them and, though I ought to be used to it by now, there's still something special about the way the thin strands appear suddenly on the sides of the drum. Like whisps of pink mist. I collect it, sweep it up on the stick in clouds that get bigger and thicker. And if there's a kid I particularly like the look of I give it an extra twirl.

The other good thing about this job (well, let's face it, any job) is it gets me out of the house. And it's funny now with all this trouble with Leri and everything, my mum doesn't keep going on about selling candy floss being common like she did when I started. She didn't approve at all. But I don't think it's got anything to do with candy floss really. She doesn't want to admit we're grown up. And I'm the baby. The last one. For her growing up means going away like John did. Though I've told her not to worry. I've got no intention of going to Saudi!

It's awful at home. Dad is always quiet anyway, but if he's not at work he's in the garden with his sweet peas and his gladioli, keeping out of the way. He just won't talk about it and that makes Mum worse. I'm sorry for her but what can I do? Leri's not in much. She spends most of her time with that Iestyn.

Mum hates him. He's got all this long black hair and beard and he's a drummer in this weird Welsh band. She says if it hadn't been for him Leri would never have got mixed up with the language lot in the first place. That's not true. All the others are with her in college and she knew them long before she ever met Iestyn.

When Leri *is* around she acts like she's a princess or something. Says we ought to be proud of her and the stand she's making. I think Mum is proud of her. In a way. She's from Tre Taliesin and you can't get more Welsh than that. Dad always says she never really settled

here though he kept hoping that she would, sooner or later. The fact that she named Leri after the river than ran at the bottom of their garden shows how homesick she was, I suppose. She's never really comfortable when she's speaking English. You can tell. But she's such a timid little person. Scared of her own shadow. And all this business with the police coming to the house and everything, it's made her that she won't go out at all and she hides behind the curtains if someone comes to the door.

As for me I'd respect Leri more if she didn't seem to love being the star of the show. I don't think she's genuine. Some of the others are. Definitely. I've listened to them talk and they've got it all worked out. They've thought it through, this business of sabotaging the computer links in the estate agents. They know what they're doing and why. Sometimes I wish I could be like that. Clear minded. Committed. Sure you're right. Leri says it's people like her that get things done. I wish I could really believe it's possible to change things. The language is important. I know that. And it's not just a question of different words for the same things. A language makes you think and feel in a special way. It makes you what you are.

But I can't help feeling it's a kind of game for Leri. She'd like to be a film star, something like that, and this is second best. Still, I'm prejudiced. I admit it. I think it would be much better if she went to Saudi and John came back.

Last night Mum started crying very quietly to herself. I sat by her on the sofa and tried to give her a hug but she only pushed me away. So I went to look for Dad in the garden. I keep telling him Mum's getting worse all the time and he really ought to do something about it. I don't know what though. She won't go to the doctor's and she won't have him come to the house. I said to Leri when she came in just to collect a dress she wanted, doesn't she ever think about the effect she's having on Mum? Leri said she was just neurotic and had always been the same. Which is true, I suppose, but so cold, so uncaring. She's like that.

It's huge, our garden. Iestyn says you could build two bungalows at least in it, but Dad bought it for the garden as a garden, not as a building site. It's the last bungalow before the Pwll y Maen estate which used to be quite nice but is awful now with half the houses boarded up and the gardens full of old cars propped up on bricks. Anyway, I stood at the top of the path and looked down towards the sea and all the lights blinking along the bay. Down there somewhere is my stripey booth with the sweet sickly smell I'm sure I'll be carrying round in my nose for the rest of my life. And then I realised something.

I like my job because it's mindless. Stops me thinking of all the trouble at home. And stops me thinking about my results. They'll be out in two weeks' time. I don't think I've done too badly and I'm sure I've done O.K. in the ones I'm going to go on with. Welsh, French and English. Like Leri.

I wonder how Daz has got on. He's clever really and he used to be great when we were in primary school. I won't be telling him Leri's court hearing's on Monday. He'll be able to read all about it in The Gazette anyway. Poor Mum. It'll kill her, that. Knowing everybody will be reading about it. I sometimes wish I could talk to Daz in an ordinary sort of way. He's alright really under all that stupid act he has to put on for the others.

It's all an act isn't it? Life, I mean. I know Dad's down there in the tool shed. He's sharpening something. I can hear the whetstone going.

As I come down the steps, it's starting to get really dark. The sun is just about to dip down in the waves, making a glitter on the water. I just wish things were different. I wish there was something I could do to make it better. If I had enough money I'd take Mum away for a holiday. Somewhere peaceful and quiet.

But you can't get away from yourself, can you?

Glenda Beagan

***

Discussion

(Read lines 10-55)
For what reasons is Daz so hostile?

*

(Read lines 55-65)
What is suggested by the remark 'It was like he was conducting an orchestra'?

*

(Read lines 65-74)
'But whose side was I on anyway?' asks Hafwen. What does she mean?

*

(Read lines 102-114)
Despite the boys' hostility, Hafwen feels that 'when they'd disappeared round the corner at last, the street looked so dull and dead'. Why might she have felt that?

*

(Read lines 115-126)
What in her use of language best expresses Hafwen's liking for her job? (Focus on at least two words or phrases.)

*

(Read lines 136-157)
In what ways is Leri different from her parents?

*

To answer the last three questions, you will need to think about the passage as a whole.

*

Describe the differing attitudes to the Welsh language indicated in these remarks:

> 'That her name, Gaz? It's something funny like that.' (line 16)
>
> 'There'd been a poor supply of laughter in our house ever since Leri'd got into the language act.' (line 83)
>
> 'A language makes you think and feel in a special way. It makes you what you are.' (line 167)

*

'It's all an act, isn't it? Life, I mean,' says Hafwen near the end of the story. What does she mean? And does she herself do any acting?

*

Imagine that you are Leri. Write a letter to a friend in which you describe your attitude to Hafwen.

Suggestions

Oral

Tell a class story. Everyone in turn has to contribute a sentence. (The title could be 'How I trained a vampire to become a decent citizen' and the first sentence 'I met him outside Woolworths'.)

If one class member was prepared to play the role of Arnold in Dylan Thomas' story then another to play Hafwen in 'Pink Summer Blues', they could answer questions (inventing where necessary) about what happens to them in the stories — and even about their lives afterwards.

In groups, discuss one of the following subjects:

Which was the best story in this section?

Who was the most memorable character?

Writing

Write a story of your choice, or else one

a) which occurs to you after looking at one of the photographs in this section.

b) in which a character sees something meant to be concealed.

c) which tells how a journey changed the lives of a group of travellers.

d) which is about a courtship that goes wrong.

e) about family relationships.

Literature

Choose one of the following. Quote briefly to illustrate your main points.

a) 'Girl meets boy...' What interested you most about the relationships between the sexes featured in 'Patricia, Edith and Arnold' and 'Pink Summer Blues'?

b) Compare and contrast 'A Midnight Gallop' and 'Patricia, Edith and Arnold' as journeys of discovery.

c) 'What every good story should have.' Give your opinion by reference to at least two of these stories.

Creatures

Words in Focus

Part of our world yet separate from it, animals have always fascinated people. They share our basic instincts, can communicate with each other. But we can barely communicate with them and, even now, know little about them. Increasingly our treatment of them is being questioned. A century from now, will we be thought of as unthinkingly cruel? 'Man is the only animal that blushes,' said Mark Twain, 'Or needs to.'

Like animals, we communicate partly through sounds, and that's a key theme of this section. When a writer describes geese as 'cackling like quarrelsome old women', for instance, he's expressing through repeated sounds (not just through words) what he hears. And he is suggesting also our divided response to animals. They can seem like people — but what are they cackling about?

Exchange

I am doing *The Red Pony*
With 3B. Despite their appetite
For murder, horror films
And modern cannibals, they
Are easily moved
By animals. Aloud, they wonder
About the first that shared our lives:
Dogs, they agree, and orphaned goats,
Suggests the girl whose mother keeps
The wholefood shop. But 'Cows, Miss?'
They do not see have anything,
Save meat and milk, to give.
So I do not try to tell them

How with the first cow that we bought,
Old, scarred and belly-sagged
With breeding, for a time I found
An old affinity, a new
Exchange. She had rosettes like flowers
Hidden in her glossy hide;
Her throat was soft as catkins
In the sun. She stood
Hock-deep in meadowsweet
Sighing as I milked her;
On winter mornings, breathed its fragrance
Through the stone cowshed. I warmed my hands
On her blackness, my heart
With her trust.

It was February, before dawn, hard frost
Squeezing the land to silence
When we loaded her. The concrete
Glistened like black slate.
It took my voice,
My hand on her flank, to get her
Stumbling up the ramp.
'Well done, Missus!' And I stood back
Smiling, as the bolts went home.
Eighty pence per kilo
On the hook. She was barren,
Useless. But I am glad
It was too dark to see her eyes.

Christine Evans

Discussion

Despite their 'appetite for murder' and other horrors, says the poet, chldren are 'easily moved' by animals. Why might this be?

*

And why are some creatures more loved than others — ponies more than cows, crane flies (Daddy-long-legs) more than spiders? They're not very different, after all.

*

What reasons does the poet give for having liked her cow so much?

*

Is 'Exchange' a good title, do you think?

*

Think about the words in the poem's last few lines. 'My hand on her flank' again — but why is it different this time?

*

If you don't know, guess what 'on the hook' means.

*

Why was the poet glad it was dark?

*

What is being suggested about the way in which we use animals in general, and how do you feel about it?

Dog

On a field like a green roof
Pitched by the sea wind
A patch of uncertain sheep
Each poised on pointed hoof
Ready for running
Stare at the coiled bitch
Alert for their turning

And stamp as she sidles
And freezes. They pick
At the steep field, they back,
Disturbing the nervous edge
Of their fleecy circle.
Slowly the bitch inches
And with a rush

Channels the stunned run.
They stream in a prim file
Through the one marked gap
In the leaning hedge,
And Fan, tongue sideways lolling,
Ushers them softly through.
Adrift on the stiff hill

The cold shepherd does not even watch them.

Leslie Norris

Discussion

Although 'Dog' is a poem in tense, short lines, its sentences are long to catch the flow of the action. Leslie Norris has chosen his words with movement in mind. There are fine visual images too, as in 'the coiled bitch', full of energy and ready to spring.

The poet has also tried to trigger another of our senses: hearing. For the sounds words make, aural images, can help us hear their meaning. A writer can make meaning more alive by choosing single words which echo what he wants to say, words that click, whisper, shuffle or rumble. Can you find such a word at the beginning of the poem's second section? 'What the words meant was of very secondary importance,' wrote Dylan Thomas about his early awakening to language. 'What mattered was the sound of them'. Say the word 'scratched', for example, and hear the sounds rub against each other, bringing echoes of scraping, screeching and scrawling.

*

A more ambitious kind of sound effect depends not on single but on repeated sounds. Of course any sentence, including this one, will contain them. Our concern is with those sounds which give meaning a voice. Having guided the sheep to the gap in the hedge, the sheep dog in Leslie Norris' poem 'ushers them softly through'. The repeated soft sound (along with the single hushing 'sh') lets the reader hear the softness he's writing about. Again, repeated sounds in 'the bitch inches' are a sort of inching forward for the ear as well as the eye and mind.

*

But not everyone will hear the same thing or interpret it in the same way. Trust your own judgement so long as you keep in mind the main purpose of sound: to enrich meaning. Read the sentence in 'Dog' beginning 'They pick...' and try to decide what effect the phrase 'the stunned run' has at its end.

*

Such techniques can work equally well in prose. Here's a sentence from one of Dylan Thomas' stories: 'Although she was the wife of my aunt, I never thought of her as anything but the wife of my uncle, partly because he was so big and trumpeting and red-hairy and used to fill every inch of the hot little house like an old buffalo squeezed into an airing cupboard, and partly because she was so small and silk and quick and made no noise at all as she whisked about on padded paws'.

*

The following poem was written originally in Welsh then translated by the author. Here are both versions.

Gwyddau

Fe'u clywid, ar drothwy'r Calan, yn gwichian yn goch
yn y stabl, a'u hadenydd yn curo'n stond
ym mhang eu hangau,
a'r gwaed, wrth ddiferu o geudwll,
yn llifo'n drochion o dan y drws.

Yn ddiniwed o'u tynged hwy,
fe'u gwelid yn torsythu ar fuarth
a chaeau'r fferm, neu'n ochri eu ffordd
yn osgordd faldorddus, hurt;
hen wyddau tafodrydd-feddw
yn clegar fel hen wragedd ffraegar mewn ffrwgwd
heb lestair ar eu parabl ystwyth,
a'u hystum yn llawn trahauster;
gwyddau wrth eu boddau mewn pydewau dwr,
neu'n pori'r maestir am oes.

Fe'u hysid fesul un
o'r cae, wrth i'r cwn
eu herlid; gwyrid y gwar
hyblyg yn lleithder y stabl,
ei wyro cyn plycio'r plu
nes bod yr wydd ddwyflwydd oed
yn gwichian a hisian fel bagbib yng nghesail
fy nhad, cyn i lafn oer
ei siswrn grafu drwy'r asgwrn yn drwsgl,
ac agor twll yn y corun.

Gerfydd eu traed rhoed y gwyddau gwarfain
i hongian yn rhengoedd
llipa a swrth; buom ninnau wrthi,
hyd hwyr y nos, yn eu trin hwy,
ac yn tynnu'r corblu o'r cyrff
nes bod y lluwchfeydd ysbeidiol yn llenwi'r lle,
a phob archoll yn staenio llawr y stabl,
a'r plu'n ymgymysgu â'r gwaed
fel ewyn gwyn gan fachlud yn goch,
ac wedi eu pluo i gyd

eu rhoi'n noeth ar y glorian wag.
Ar doriad y wawr
drannoeth, yr oedd llwydrew Ionawr
fel plu yn gwaedu i gyd.

Geese

On New Year's Eve, one could hear their red scream
in the stable, and the wings beating still
in the grasp of death,
and the blood, dripping from a round hole,
flowed like foam under the door.

Innocent of their fate,
they could be seen swaggering on the farmyard
and on the fields, or waddling
in a stupid, babbling host;
loose-tongued, drunken geese
cackling like quarrelsome old women,
their supple speech without restraint,
and their postures arrogant;
geese grazing the fields for a lifetime
or paddling in pools.

One by one they would be pursued
from the field, set on by dogs;
the flexible nape would be bent
in the damp stable,
bent before the feathers were plucked,
and the young goose
hissed and screamed like bagpipes in my father's
armpit, before the cold blade
of his scissors scraped clumsily through the bone,
and opened a hole in the head.

The thin-naped geese dangled by their feet
as limp as clothes on the clothes-line;
it took us to nightfall
plucking the feathers and scorching the skin,
and the snatched snow grew on the ground;
the stable's floor was stained by wounds,

and the feathers, mingling with the blood,
were as white foam fuming red in the sunset,
and scoured, they were placed on the scales.
On the break of dawn the next day
the hoarfrost of January
bled like feathers.

Alan Llwyd

***

Discussion

Just past the halfway point, Alan Llwyd could have written 'his scissors pushed awkwardly through the bone'. Instead he wrote 'his scissors *scraped* clumsily through the bone'. Decide which version you prefer and why.

*

Of these three, which sound do you find easiest to describe?

'flowed like foam under the door'

'paddling in pools'

'white foam fuming red'

*

Try this yourself. Think of helpful repeated sounds in a phrase about thunder overhead or rain falling on a pavement. (Sounds can be the same even when their letters aren't, as in the noisily quacking 'c' sounds in 'cackling like quarrelsome old women' in Alan Llwyd's poem.)

*

Apart from the words quoted so far, which single ones echoing their meanings can you hear most clearly in the poem? Can you find any in the Welsh version of the poem?

*

Usually sound is used to sharpen visual images. The reverse is true in the first line though: a visual image is used to capture a sound. Imagine what the poet had in mind in that line: 'one could hear their red scream'.

*

The repeated 's' sound can be very useful, as in the hiss of burning in 'scorching the skin'. Try thinking of a phrase about a small animal moving in the grass or a bird in the leaves, bringing their sounds alive.

*

Rhyme is another technique appealing to the ear. It can be a musical chiming as one line echoes another or, in comic verse, provide an emphatic snap. When you read the poem 'Pastoral', by Emyr Humphreys, notice how the triple rhymes give a confident firmness to what's being said.

Voices

Horses

Suddenly there were forms there:
Heads bright of eye
Leapt out of the alien dark,
Out of the night into the headlights' gleam.

The twentieth century braked
And in the tousled manes before us
Pieces out of the past were
Gazing at us brightly.

Neighing and snorting nostrils,
Legs teeming with terror;
Scattering then. After the hooves
Stopped threshing the darkness: stillness.

After the nerves of seeing
Stopped twitching with the imprint of the flurry
Of the forms that came before our faces
Like a fist, the light was full of quietness.

Shifting into gear and moving
On a road that wound along the face of the world
In a wide night where time was untied
And let loose in a fearful roaming.

Gwyn Thomas
(trans: Joseph Clancy)

Pastoral

This morning, yawning, Dic Fawr said
'Evans the *Ship and Castle* is dead'
'Is he indeed? Poor chap,' I said.

The huge horse rose in its shadowy stall
We smoked and watched its brown excreta fall
And Dic said, spitting, 'After all

You couldn't expect a chap like that
With bottles to hand from where he sat
Not to soak. His belly was like a vat.'

Dic went across to stir the horse's feed.
'Come on. Eat up,' he said, 'you're harrowing the
fifteen acre field
All day today,' and wistfully to me, 'It was a nice
death indeed.'

Outside the lark was gargling with dew
When Dic led out Captain Belle and True
The sunlight dripped in the lane. The sky was blue.

Emyr Humphreys

The Computer's First Proverbs

after Edwin Morgan

You can take a dog to the keyside, but you can't push him in
all is wet that starts to bark
if you pay peanuts you get them planted in the park
nothing should be done in haste but grip your trout
if you want fish, you must prepare for stink
he who fishes with the piper barks like a dog
he who fishes a tiger is afraid to wink
fish will out, fish will out
all roaring is the same in the dark.

A dog in the brook is worth avoiding
think of a fountain and you froth in the head
speech is water, fish are water
it is too late to rub in embrocation after the dream has gone
strike while the law is out
put the stout dog to a deaf oven
flush the fridge if you have a long arm
idle lips make the best smoke rings
fishmongers always make room
it is all melted than ends melted
in May let the plugs bloom
You cannot roar with the workers and ignore the phone
it takes three waders to make a wet man
the longest dog winks all the way home

Peter Finch

(An improvisation on the Oxford Dictionary of Proverbs)

Pig-killing day

I watched from the bedroom, all sound
from out there jammed by the music
that boomed inside.
                                        Then up
from the beech-tops the rooks
unfurled, hung streaming
through dull white sky,
        till a peace below
                drew them filtering back,
and someone turned down the broadcast.

They dragged her from the trailer
like some damaged drunk, his
nakedness snarled with red string,
and in the outhouse where
we'd stewed her spuds, they
hooked her up, paunch taut
for the knife's first nagging.

Heads above bowls
crossed the yard
                                    all day
as they scraped and scalded,
hacked and subtracted, slowly
spreading the room with pig.

The kitchen by evening was plump
with faggots and strange other
pieces.

All that remained
of the pig I'd known lay uncurled
in the coal hod, brightened with dust.
They said me goodnight, with their
clean hands brushed me...

We ate well of the pig, she
lasted us months
though for days
I preferred to ride on the tractor, shy
of the trailer, the death
it brought home.

Nigel Jenkins

Manawyddan

The Mabinogion is the title used by Charlotte Guest for her translations of twelve mediaeval Welsh tales. This extract is from the story of Manawyddan.

And one morning Pryderi and Manawyddan rose up to hunt, and they ranged their dogs and went forth from the palace. And some of the dogs ran before them and came to a small bush which was near at hand; but as soon as they were come to the bush, they hastily drew back and returned to the men, their hair bristling up greatly. 'Let us go near to the bush,' said Pryderi, 'and see what is in it.' And as they came near, behold, a wild boar of a pure white colour rose up from the bush. Then the dogs, being set on by the men, rushed towards him; but he left the bush and fell back a little way from the men, and made a stand against the dogs without retreating from them, until the men had come near. And when the men came up, he fell back a second time, and betook him to flight. Then they pursued the boar until they beheld a vast and lofty castle, all newly built, in a place where they had never before seen either stone or building. And the boar ran swiftly into the castle and the dogs after him. Now when the boar and the dogs had gone into the castle, they began to wonder at finding a castle in a place where they had never before seen any building whatsoever. And from the top of the Gorsedd they looked and listened for the dogs. But so long as they were there they heard not one of the dogs nor aught concerning them.

'Lord,' said Pryderi, 'I will go into the castle to get tidings of the dogs.' 'Truly,' he replied, 'thou wouldst be unwise to go into this castle, which thou hast never seen till now. If thou wouldst follow my counsel, thou wouldst not enter therein. Whosoever has cast a spell over this land has caused this castle to be here.' 'Of a truth,' answered Pryderi, 'I cannot thus give up my dogs.' And for all the counsel that Manawyddan gave him, yet to the castle he went.

When he came within the castle, neither man nor beast, nor boar nor dogs, nor house, nor dwelling saw he within it. But in the centre of the castle floor he beheld a fountain with marble work around it, and on the margin of the fountain a golden bowl upon a marble slab, and chains hanging from the air, to which he saw no end. And he was greatly pleased with the beauty of the gold, and with the rich workmanship of the bowl, and he went up to the bowl and laid hold of it. And when he had taken hold of it his hands stuck to the bowl, and his feet to the slab on which the bowl was placed, and all his joyousness forsook him, so that he could not utter a word. And thus he stood.

And Manawyddan waited for him till near the close of the day. And late in the evening, being certain that he should have no tidings of Pryderi or of the dogs, he went back to the palace. And as he entered, Rhiannon looked at him. 'Where,' said she, 'are thy companion and thy dogs?' 'Behold,' he answered, 'the adventure that has befallen me.' And he related it all unto her. 'An evil companion hast thou been,' said Rhiannon, 'and a good companion hast thou lost.' And with that word she went out, and proceeded towards the castle according to the direction which he gave her. The gate of the castle she found open. She was nothing daunted, and she went in. And as she went in, she perceived Pryderi laying hold of the bowl, and she went towards him. 'Oh, my lord,' said she, 'what dost thou do here?' And she took hold of the bowl with him; and as she did so her hands became fast to the bowl, and her feet to the slab, and she was not able to utter a word. And with that, as it became night, lo, there came thunder upon them, and a fall of mist, and thereupon the castle vanished, and they with it.

***

Barn Owl

Ernie Morgan found him, a small
Fur mitten inexplicably upright,
And hissing like a treble kettle
Beneath the tree he'd fallen from.
His bright eye frightened Ernie,
Who popped a rusty bucket over him
And ran for us. We kept him
In a backyard shed, perched
On the rung of a broken deck-chair,
Its canvas faded to his down's biscuit.
Men from the pits, their own childhood
Spent waste in the crippling earth,
Held him gently, brought him mice
From the wealth of our riddled tenements,
Saw that we understood his tenderness,
His tiny body under its puffed quilt,
Then left us alone. We called him Snowy.

He was never clumsy. He flew
From the first like a skilled moth,
Sifting the air with feathers,
Floating it softly to the place he wanted.
At dusk he'd stir, preen, stand
At the window-ledge, fly. It was
A catching of the heart to see him go.
Six months we kept him, saw him
Grow beautiful in a way each thought
His own knowledge. One afternoon, home
With pretended illness, I watched him
Leave. It was daylight. He lifted slowly
Over the Hughes's roof, his cream face calm,
And never came back. I saw this;
And tell it for the first time,
Having wanted to keep his mystery.

And would not say it now, but that
This morning, walking in Slindon woods
Before the sun, I found a barn owl
Dead in the rusty bracken.

He was not clumsy in his death,
His wings folded decently to him,
His plumes, unruffled orange,
Bore flawlessly their delicate patterning.

With a stick I turned him, not
Wishing to touch his feathery stiffness.
There was neither blood nor wound on him,
But for the savaged foot a scavenger
Had ripped. I saw the sinews.
I could have skewered them out
Like a common fowl's. Moving away
I was oppressed by him, thinking
Cofusedly that down the generations
Of air this death was Snowy's
Emblematic messenger, that I should know
The meaning of it, the dead barn owl.

Leslie Norris

Porpoise

The sea spreads beaten metal
to the earth's edge,

my head full of thunder
and the hot rims of clouds.

The sea splits
to the rolling of porpoise

one
another
then another,

wheels of sky and water

I point,
a dumb animal on the prom,

I watch their fleshy sails
turn south

leaving a patch of light.

Gwyn Parry

Discussion

The story of *Manawyddan* reminds us of the mystery, the strangeness, of animal life. What evidence of it have you found in the poems you've read so far?

*

Poems about creatures are often about people too. What kind of animal is the human being on the evidence of what you've read?

*

With which of the seven poems about creatures do you think 'Pig-killing Day' has most in common?

*

Can you find any interesting use of word sounds in Leslie Norris' poem 'Barn Owl'?

*

Which of the two poems do you prefer? Why?

*

Gwyn Parry's poem 'Porpoise' doesn't have the detail of some other poems in this section. What does it offer instead?

The Saddist

'He were squirming. He were. He were coming straight for me.'

There is an austere pleasure to be found in porcelain and scouring powder, the clean smell, the grittiness. Not for Mrs Mossop those new-fangled detergent creams. She prefers the old-fashioned stuff, the kind that requires the liberal application of elbow grease. Mine. Hovering explosively at the door she is determined that nothing will divert her narrative flow. The bath needs cleaning, yes, but not as much as her story needs telling.

'He were huge. HUGE. At least a foot long. And in all that rain he were swimming up the path. You should've seen him.'

Swimming. Squirming. I practise my Buddhist detachment. I observe my right arm describe a circle on the pitted surface. Now I concentrate on the stained patches under the taps. Nothing will stop her. She prods me on the shoulder, insistent, and then with an arthritic creak she half-kneels beside me.

'Are you listening? I'm telling you.'

I stop. I must. There is no other way. I stand up, wipe the sweat off my face. How humid it is. Last night's rain, torrential, hours of it. And now this heat. This stuffy little house. Jungle weather.

'He were horrible.'

She pauses, gratified. She now has my full attention.

'Was he an eel or something?'

'Don't know what he were. Like a long worm. Thick, inches of him. And he were squirming.'

So am I. So is she. She is upright again, clutching my hand, pushing her face into mine.

'I were cruel,' she says, her voice suddenly fading. And I realise she is afraid and not of the worm, the eel, whatever it was. Of something else. There is a strange hush in the bathroom, broken for a moment by ice-cream chimes far away.

'I'm a saddist.'

It sounds worse said like that. Absurd. Incongruous. The look on her face. What can I make of it? Relish. Fear. Pride. Shame. A medley. A darkness.

'What did you do?'

I sit on the side of the bath, my face assuming a mask, of what, tolerance, acceptance? What will she say?

'Come and have a look. Come on. In the kitchen.'

I follow, across the boxy hall with its scrap of rug. Orange green swirls.

'Here.'

She stops, pointing at the door into her small square garden. It's open, propped back with a stone.

'Look.'

I look. Nothing. Only the path, the clothes line, two towels and a puce-coloured blouse. The dust bin, the hedge. Beyond it the church tower, the new weather-vane, a gilded fish. It isn't spinning today. The scene is static. The air is static.

'He were there.'

We stand at the door now, looking out at the blandness. It doesn't match. I half expect a monster to materialise before me. Perhaps it has.

'It were the rain,' she says, 'It were hammering. Something in it. He were horrible and I couldn't stand it.' She looks up at me. 'I couldn't.' She has a fine sense of theatre, has Mrs Mossop.

'So what did you do?'

'I got the salt.'

She moves over to the cupboard. Stuck on with browned curling sellotape are postcards. Ibiza. Weston-super-Mare. She opens the door. Among cans and soup packets a large earthenware pot. She gets it out, holds it, large eyed, as if cradling Aladdin's lamp.

'This.'

She pokes it under my nose.

'Look.' I do.

'There's hardly any left.'

'No. I used it all. It were nearly full. On him. To stop him squirming. Stop him coming into the house. 'Cos he were coming. Definite. Coming straight for me.'

I gulp.

'I kept pouring it on him. Out there.'

She nods towards the door. Grimaces. Half shuts her eyes. I see it all now. The rain, the darkness, Mrs Mossop in her pom-pom slippers, a huddled form, the thing on the path in the light from the door. And then the salt. Scooped out. Handful after handful. Then poured. Then panic.

'He were squirming like a mad thing so I kept piling it on him. But it were raining, of course, so it kept melting.'

'Melting?'

'Yes, like a steam were coming off him.'

She rubs her fingernail on the rim of the pot. Finds a crusted bit. Scratches at it.

'Then he stopped squirming.'

Now she's sat herself on the straight-backed chair by the cooker.

'He were really dead. I checked. I poked him with a stick. There was mountains of salt on him.'

She shudders. 'My sister always said...'

'What?'

'That I were cruel.'

I'm supposed to be cleaning. I haven't even finished the bathroom yet and I'm supposed to be at Mrs Sellingham's by three o'clock. What is all this? Is it real? Another of Mrs Mossop's stalling devices? Always a new story, a new snatch of gossip. But this time it's different.

'She said I were cruel. And I were. I used to kill things. Not just in the house, like a wasp or something. No. Outside too. Things that weren't doing me no harm at all.'

A pause. 'What sort of things?'

'All sorts of things. Ladybirds. Butterflies. Things you're supposed to like. I used to catch the butterflies on the bush by Miss Webb's wall. She were the teacher. I took some to school in a jar one day. She didn't know where from. Put them on her nature table. I drew them in my book after. Red Admirals she said they were.'

She is far away. How many years? Sixty? Seventy?

'And I *mean* kill 'em. Not just let them die. Slowly. Like I said I'm a saddist.' It's very quiet here. No traffic. No ice-cream chimes. Nothing. The last in a row of boxy little houses under the church at the edge of town. She sniffs.

'But it weren't just insects.'

'No?'

'No. When I were married, not long married, I mean the second time, 'cos, my first husband, Cyril, he left, we moved into the new council houses. Nice big houses they were too, but the garden was just meadow, you understand. Never been anything grown there, so Bert dug it all out and planted potatoes to start it off. He worked that hard, he did. Kept a lovely garden.'

'Yes?'

'And I were helping him clear it out one day, down in the longgrass and it were damp at the far end. And we had a bonfire for all the dried stuff we'd cleared out before. When I found him.'

'What?'

'A bullfrog. He were a whopper. Like one of them dinosaurs. And I got him on my spade and I were going to chuck him in the fire.'

She clutches the salt pot tighter.

'Bert grabbed the spade off me. He were shocked. You could tell. He said, Lily, you weren't going to burn 'im? Not really? And I said, No. Course not. But I were. I were that ashamed after, the way Bert looked at me. As if he couldn't stand the sight of me. He took that frog down to the pond on the other side of the railway. And I felt he were never the same with me after that. Never.'

She rubs the top button on her cardigan. Baby-blue wool. Pearl button. I glance at my watch surreptitiously. She notices.

'You got to go in a minute?'

'Yes. And I haven't finished the bathroom yet.'

'Never mind. You go to that Mrs Sellingham's after me?'

I nod. A flicker of interest. A wash of change.

'What's she like?'

What do I say? I hover. Suddenly I want to put my arms round Mrs Mossop, hug her, tell her she's not a sadist. That there are all kinds of cruelty in the world and among the many cruelties hers are very small indeed. I could tell her about Mrs Sellingham, couldn't I? The perfect lady in her big house with the stained glass and the fanlight. I don't. I pat her on the hand. Mutter something conciliatory. Pointless.

She sits there. Stares hard at the pans on the shelf.

'Last week it were the snails. On the path that comes down from the precinct, past that big carpet place. There was hundreds of them. I crunched them. I were wearing my new shoes, the ones that pinch, and I went stamping on them, slithering them. Like a jelly all over the path.'

I reach for my coat, thinly, as if trying not to move, to go.

'I don't know why I do it.' She looks me straight in the eye. 'I don't want to be cruel. But I always have been. Always.'

'We all are sometimes,' I say feebly. 'And anyway, there are lots of people who are cruel all the time, much more cruel than you, and they don't even know they're doing it.'

'I know I'm doing it.'

I take the salt pot from her, put it back in the cupboard.

Glenda Beagan

***

Discussion

What do you think Mrs Mossop saw on her garden path?

*

'She has a fine sense of theatre, Mrs Mossop,' says the writer. What does she mean?

*

Why does Mrs Mossop tell her visitors this story, do you think?

*

'I half expect a monster to materialize before me. Perhaps it has.' Would you describe Mrs Mossop as a cruel person? Why did she do what she did?

*

How would you sum-up her visitor's reaction to Mrs Mossop's confession?

Weasels

They are only scraps for a furrier
or trimming for a lady's wrap.
But before they end on a heap
they are awful in the fields and streams.
Red-brown and nine inches long,
they eat mice and moles and frogs;
rooks, crows and owls are nothing to them.
Weasels will get through a bush or hedge
for thrush and blackbird eggs
and swim a mile when they sniff dead fish.

My grandad saw one
wipe out a granary of rats
and then look around to see
if he had missed any
before he enjoyed his huge supper.
Once, in America, a hawk was found
with a weasel's skull locked to its throat.
Even when chased by a fox
they may stop to kill a chicken.
Weasels like rabbits, too
and go deep into the dark burrows.
In Carmarthen they have hunted in packs
scampering behind the poor scared hares
lolloping in the moonlight.
They will also attack a man
if trapped — single and alone
they jump for the neck.

Weasels will live anywhere smelly:
inside a maggoty sheep carcase
or a rotted tree-stump,
a crumbled wall crevice or a fish hole
in the riverbank. Their innocent babies
nest tight at the back of the holes.

John Tripp

I am Taliesin. I sing perfect r

I am Taliesin. I sing perfect metre,
Which will last to the end of the world.
My patron is Elphin...

I know why there is an echo in a hollow;
Why silver gleams; why breath is black; why l
Why a cow has horns; why a woman is affecti
Why milk is white; why holly is green;
Why a kid is bearded; why the cow-parsnip is
Why brine is salt; why ale is bitter;
Why the linnet is green and berries red;
Why a cuckoo complains; why it sings;
I know where the cuckoos of summer are in
I know what beasts there are at the bottom of the sea,
How many spears in battle; how many drops in a shower;
Why a river drowned Pharaoh's people;
Why fishes have scales,
Why a white swan has black feet...

I have been a blue salmon,
I have been a dog, a stag, a roebuck on the mountain,
A stock, a spade, an axe in the hand,
A stallion, a bull, a buck,
A grain which grew on a hill,
I was reaped, and placed in an oven,
I fell to the ground when I was being roasted
And a hen swallowed me.
For nine nights was I in her crop.
I have been dead, I have been alive,
I am Taliesin.

Anonymous, 13th century
(trans. Sir Ifor Williams)

Suggestions

Oral

'Animals are our necessary servants': a class debate. There could be two speakers on each side, a chairperson, and contributions from the audience could follow those of the main speakers.

Prose

Draw on your own experience for a piece of writing entitled 'Some Encounters with Animals'.

Imagine yourself as a creature. Where are you? What can you see? Why are you moving forward now?

Outline your opinions about people and animals in response to the issues raised by the topic for debate mentioned above.

Write a story involving animal life — possibly in response to one of the photographs in this section, or write a mythical story like 'Manawyddan'.

Poetry

Write notes for a poem about an animal or bird, trying to 'see' your subject through fresh images. If it's a cat, what are its ears like? How exactly could you describe its head? Of what does its drifting tail remind you? And, if possible, think about word sounds so the reader will hear sometimes as well as see. (How would you capture a cat's purring? Its quiet passage through undergrowth?)

*

Glance again at 'I am Taliesin'. Write a poem in which you use your own name in the title 'I am — ' and beginning some lines with 'I know' or 'I have been'.

Write a poem about a waterfall or a river in flood, alive with sounds. If you were writing about the sea, for instance, you could begin:

> The rough sea grinds
> stones and shells
> to a silky sand...

*

Could you imagine a computer producing 'The Computer's First Proverbs'? Write your own computer poem.

Rhyme is a useful aural technique. Rhymes in pairs, rhyming couplets, can add comic emphasis to a light poem. Try one about an animal, sounding conversationally relaxed as you run from line to line, something like:

> The hedgehog scuttled out of sleep at last
> and we watched him, a drunk, staggering past

Literature

You have been asked to produce some video film to accompany readings of two or three poems about creatures. Describe what you film, being as inventive as possible. Don't forget to quote, to show which of the poets' lines you have in mind.

Write letters to one or two of the poets, saying what has interested you in their work (you needn't be wholly enthusiastic), and including questions if you like.

Compare and contrast two poems, either 'Pastoral' and 'Horses' or 'Geese' and 'Pig-killing day'.

Dialogues

When Dylan Thomas's play for voices, *Under Milk Wood*, was first broadcast by the BBC in 1954, it set a new standard for radio drama. Listeners were invited by a writer fascinated not just by the meanings of words — 'what mattered was the sound of them' — to 'Listen...come closer now' to a small Welsh coastal town and its inhabitants. The play opens at night when sound reigns over vision. We meet Captain Cat who, blind, has to rely on what he can hear. And although listeners are invited to 'Look' too, it is sounds which most capture the listener's imagination, all 'the seaslides of saying'. Along with an excerpt from *Under Milk Wood*, two others from recent radio plays are included here. More spare in their use of language, more realistic in approach, Greg Cullen and Charles Way reveal in their different ways the power of dialogue to open telephone lines from people's minds. Not just through what people say or half-say but also through their way of saying it, we hear their thoughts. They may not be what they say they are.

Funny Boys

The two main characters in this play are Tom and his partner Owain (whose stage name is Twp). They are a comedy duo who started in the Cardiff clubs and are slowly climbing the show business ladder. The period is the nineteen-sixties. In this extract, Tom is walking at night along Blackpool pier with his girl friend, Anwen, who can speak Welsh, unlike Tom.

TOM: Are we going to walk to the very end?

ANWEN: Why not? That's where the titles come up.

TOM: I tell the jokes! I mean, do we have to walk to the end? Before you can say what you came out here to say —

ANWEN: I thought it would be nice to go for a walk together—

TOM: Oh aye — it is— very.

ANWEN: I don't know what I see in you. We've got nothing in common.

TOM: We're not even the same sex.

ANWEN: Don't you ever stop performing?

TOM: Only when I'm eating. You couldn't afford to tell jokes in our house. Some other brat would have the food off your plate — you think I'm joking, don't you?

ANWEN: Oh come here, you big softie.

TOM: That's more like it. Lights glittering on the blue-black water, music drifting across the moonlit bay — what have we got?

ANWEN: Romance.

TOM: Four kids and a twin-tub.

(They laugh) (Kiss)

ANWEN: Come on, we'll get a better view of the illuminations further along.

TOM: Bloody hell. It's like walking to the Isle of Man. By the time we get back, the front will be packed with punters you know

ANWEN: So, you'll love it. You can strut like you normally do.

TOM: I never strut.

ANWEN: Course you do, all those people staring, wanting autographs — you strut.

TOM: It's what they want, to gawp at the stars from the gutter.

ANWEN: I think you really believe that.

TOM: You're just jealous.

ANWEN: Maybe. I wish to God I wasn't. O dwyn mas o'm gof.

TOM: What's that then?

ANWEN: I must be mad.

TOM: Why?

ANWEN: To be with you.

TOM: Certifiably. Well, here we are then. Good God, that's a lot of light bulbs. Magic, hey. I love lights — ever since I worked down the Pit, lights have a special meaning.

ANWEN: Owain says they look trashy.

TOM: He would.

ANWEN: Is he alright?

TOM: Do we have to talk about Owain? He's homesick that's all. His body's in Blackpool but his heart's in Blackwood. One step out of Wales and he comes up in a rash. He'll grow out of it. He's got to, it's a long season.

ANWEN: Doesn't he enjoy the show?

TOM: Course. They love him up here, the cuddly Celt. Everywhere he goes the punters shout, — 'Hello Mam!' He laps it up. They even give him a laugh when he sings his little song in Welsh. Very generous, I thought.

ANWEN: Very.

(She walks away)

TOM: (Goes after her) Don't get me wrong. It's a short song, that's all I meant and the Brums don't understand a word but they still applaud. That's generous, that's all I'm saying. Anwen, why did you bring me out here?

ANWEN: I want to push you off the pier.

TOM: Don't you love me anymore?

ANWEN: No.

TOM: You don't know what you feel. That's your trouble, you and Owain. Come on Anwen, much as I love the sea air, the smell of candy-floss and ageing Teddy Boys — I'm getting cold.

ANWEN: I've been offered a job.

TOM: Great. Who for and how much?

ANWEN: It's a new Welsh Language Theatre Company.

TOM: Oh well, never mind.

ANWEN: Listen! It's a fairly long commitment, which means I won't be able to do any more radio shows.

TOM: Anwen, wake up mun. What chance have you got touring the outback in Welsh? Who's going to spot talent out there? —- George Borrow? Stick with us, we've got Holiday Town Parade on the tele, you can be part of it — same as on the radio. Don't go throwing yourself away in some dead-end job.

ANWEN: I said yes.

TOM: You are mad. You are stark raving mad. Oh sorry, forgot, you want to be a starving actress in 'The Theatre' — variety's a dirty word. You're making a mistake.

ANWEN: Then it's my mistake. I've already said yes, so I don't need your advice.

TOM: So what do you want to tell me for, for Christ's sake — say it.

ANWEN: I won't be seeing much of you. Not that I have been anyway.

TOM: So.

ANWEN: It makes me wonder about us. I'm sick and tired of these long argumentative weekends in grotty seaside resorts.

TOM: Listen. We'll be back in the autumn. We've got six radios in Cardiff and the panto at Swansea Grand. We'd never miss that. Owen loves it. So we'll be home on the ruddy range and we'll see each other.

ANWEN: It's not enough.

TOM: All we need is something strong, to keep us together while we're apart. Until Twp and I make it really big and then we can pick and choose when we work, we'll have all the time in the world. I was thinking — we could get married.

ANWEN: Oh, Tom.

TOM: It may help us persevere like.

ANWEN: I don't know, maybe, I don't know.

TOM: Time to go — the show must go on.

ANWEN: As usual.

(Fade)

Charles Way

***

Discussion

A writer of dialogue has to be able to suggest, through the order and choice of words, how they should be spoken. There can be little description as there is in short stories...'she said gloomily'. When Anwen says 'I thought it would be nice to go for a walk together', for instance, and Tom answers 'Oh aye — it is— very', we're led by his short, broken-up reply to guess that he is not convinced. What tones of voice do you hear in the snatches of dialogue below?

TOM: They even give him a laugh when he sings his little song in Welsh. Very generous, I thought.

ANWEN: Very.

*

ANWEN: I've said yes.

TOM: You are mad...Oh sorry, forgot, you want to be a starving actress in 'The Theatre'...

*

TOM: I was thinking — we could get married.

ANWEN: Oh, Tom.

*

By the end of the extract, what conclusions have you drawn about the cause of the tension between the two? And is Owain (Twp) closer to Anwen's way of thinking or Tom's?

*

Write a piece of dialogue for radio (tape recording) based on one of these situations — or think of your own. Write only what can be heard not things seen or thought. And as soon as possible, the speakers should indicate to the listener who they are and what their relationship is.

a)A group of reluctant teenagers is given a careers talk by an Army officer. As the extract opens, his talk is coming to an end — then he invites questions.

b) A couple soon to be married are being shown around an unoccupied house by a keen estate agent. One of the couple is enthusiastic, the other isn't. (The house owners could arrive during the meeting's final stages.)

c) Think of an interesting situation involving a blind man or woman.

In groups now, choose one script by a group member and plan to read it, sharing ideas about tones of voice, pauses, possible sound effects.

Under Milk Wood

A Play for Voices

Dylan Thomas' radio play, set in a small Welsh town by a sea of fantasies, includes:

FIRST VOICE
SECOND VOICE
MR PRITCHARD
MR OGMORE
MRS OGMORE-PRITCHARD
MR PUGH
MRS PUGH

FIRST VOICE: Now, in her iceberg-white, holily laundered crinoline nightgown, under virtuous polar sheets, in her spruced and scoured dust-defying bedroom in trig and trim Bay View, a house for paying guests, at the top of the town, Mrs Ogmore-Pritchard widow, twice, of Mr Ogmore, linoleum, retired, and Mr Pritchard, failed bookmaker, who maddened by besoming, swabbing and scrubbing, the voice of the vacuum-cleaner and the fume of polish, ironically swallowed disinfectant, fidgets in her rinsed sleep, wakes in a dream, and nudges in the ribs dead Mr Ogmore, dead Mr Pritchard, ghostly on either side.

MRS OGMORE-PRITCHARD: Mr Ogmore! Mr Pritchard! It is time to inhale your balsam.

MR OGMORE: Oh, Mrs Ogmore!

MR PRITCHARD: Oh, Mrs Pritchard!

MRS OGMORE-PRITCHARD: Soon it will be time to get up. Tell me your tasks, in order.

MR OGMORE: I must put my pyjamas in the drawer marked pyjamas.

MR PRITCHARD: I must take my cold bath which is good for me.

MR OGMORE: I must wear my flannel band to ward off sciatica.

MR PRITCHARD: I must dress behind the curtain and put on my apron.

MR OGMORE: I must blow my nose.

MRS OGMORE-PRITCHARD: In the garden, if you please.

MR OGMORE: In a piece of tissue-paper which I afterwards burn.

MR PRITCHARD: I must take my salts which are nature's friend.

MR OGMORE: I must boil the drinking water because of germs.

MR PRITCHARD: I must make my herb tea which is free from tannin.

MR OGMORE: And have a charcoal biscuit which is good for me.

MR PRITCHARD: I may smoke one pipe of asthma mixture.

MRS OGMORE-PRITCHARD: In the woodshed, if you please.

MR PRITCHARD: And dust the parlour and spray the canary.

MR OGMORE: I must put on rubber gloves and search the peke for fleas.

MR PRITCHARD: I must dust the blinds and then I must raise them.

MRS OGMORE-PRITCHARD: And before you let the sun in, mind it wipes its shoes.

FIRST VOICE: In the blind-drawn dark dining-room of School House, dusty and echoing as a dining-room in a vault, Mr and Mrs Pugh are silent over cold grey cottage pie. Mr Pugh reads, as he forks the shroud meat in, from *Lives of the Great Poisoners*. He has bound a plain brown-paper cover round the book. Slyly, between slow mouthfuls, he sidespies up at Mrs Pugh, poisons her with his eye, then goes on reading. He underlines certain passages and smiles in secret.

MRS PUGH: Persons with manners do not read at table,

FIRST VOICE: says Mrs Pugh. She swallows a digestive tablet as big as a horse-pill, washing it down with clouded peasoup water.

(Pause)

MRS PUGH: Some persons were brought up in pigsties.

MR PUGH: Pigs don't read at table, dear.

FIRST VOICE: Bitterly she flicks dust from the broken cruet. It settles on the pie in a thin gnat-rain.

MR PUGH: Pigs can't read, my dear.

MRS PUGH: I know one that can.

FIRST VOICE: Alone in the hissing laboratory of his wishes, Mr Pugh minces among bad vats and jeroboams, tiptoes through spinneys of murdering herbs, agony dancing in his crucibles, and mixes especially for Mrs Pugh a venomous porridge unknown to toxicologists which will scald and viper through her until her ears fall off like figs, her toes grow big and black as balloons, and steam comes screaming out of her navel.

MR PUGH: It's a theological work, my dear. *Lives of the Great Saints.*

FIRST VOICE: Mrs Pugh smiles. An icicle forms in the cold air of the dining-vault.

MRS PUGH: I saw you talking to a saint this morning. Saint Polly Garter. She was martyred again last night. Mrs Organ Morgan saw her with Mr Waldo.

FIRST VOICE: The sunny slow lulling afternoon yawns and moons through the dozy town. The sea lolls, laps and idles in, with fishes sleeping in its lap. The meadows still as Sunday, the shut-eye tasselled bulls, the goat-and-daisy dingles, nap happy and lazy. The dumb duck-ponds snooze. Clouds sag and pillow on Llareggub Hill. Pigs grunt in a wet wallow-bath, and smile as they snort and dream. They dream of the acorned swill of the world, the rooting for pig-fruit, the bagpipe dugs of the mother sow, the squeal and snuffle of yesses of the women pigs in rut. They mud-bask and snout in the pig-loving sun; their tails curl; they rollick and slobber and snore to deep, smug, after-swill sleep. Donkeys angelically drowse on Donkey Down.

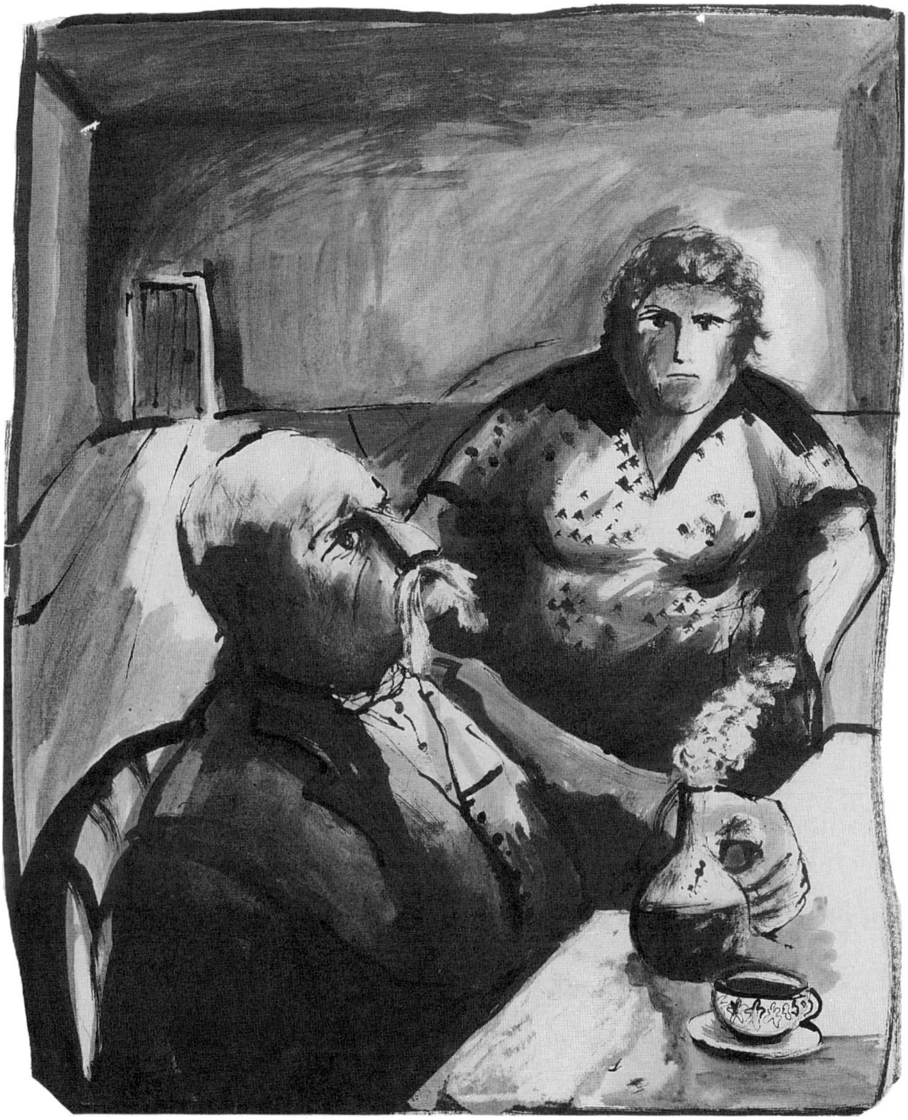

MRS PUGH: Persons with manners,

SECOND VOICE: snaps Mrs cold Pugh,

MRS PUGH: do not nod at table.

FIRST VOICE: Mr Pugh cringes awake. He puts on a soft-soaping smile: it is sad and grey under his nicotine-eggyellow weeping walrus Victorian moustache worn thick and long in memory of Doctor Crippen.

MRS PUGH: You should wait until you retire to your sty,

SECOND VOICE: says Mrs Pugh, sweet as a razor. His fawning measly quarter-smile freezes. Sly and silent, he foxes into his chemist's den and there, in a hiss and prussic circle of cauldrons and phials brimful with pox and the Black Death, cooks up a fricassee of deadly nightshade, nicotine, hot frog, cyanide and bat-spit for his needling stalactite hag and bednag of a pokerbacked nutcracker wife.

MR PUGH: I beg your pardon, my dear,

SECOND VOICE: he murmurs with a wheedle.

FIRST VOICE: Now the town is dusk. Each cobble, donkey, goose and gooseberry street is a thoroughfare of dusk; and dusk and ceremonial dust, and night's first darkening snow, and the sleep of birds, drift under and through the live dusk of this place of love. Llareggub is the capital of dusk.

Mrs Ogmore-Pritchard, at the first drop of the dusk-shower, seals all her sea-view doors, draws the germ-free blinds, sits, erect as a dry dream on a high-backed hygienic chair and wills herself to cold, quick sleep. At once, at twice, Mr Ogmore and Mr Pritchard, who all dead day long have been gossiping like ghosts in the woodshed, planning the loveless destruction of their glass widow, reluctantly sigh and sidle into her clean house.

MR PRITCHARD: You first, Mr Ogmore.

MR OGMORE: After you, Mr Pritchard.

MR PRITCHARD: No, no, Mr Ogmore. You widowed her first.

FIRST VOICE: And in through the keyhole, with tears where their eyes once were, they ooze and grumble.

MRS OGMORE-PRITCHARD: Husbands,

FIRST VOICE: she says in her sleep. There is acid love in her voice for one of the two shambling phantoms. Mr Ogmore hopes that it is not for him. So does Mr Pritchard.

MRS OGMORE-PRITCHARD: I love you both.

MR OGMORE: (With terror) Oh, Mrs Ogmore.

MR PRITCHARD: (With horror) Oh, Mrs Pritchard.

MRS OGMORE-PRITCHARD: Soon it will be time to go to bed. Tell me your tasks in order.

MR OGMORE AND MR PRITCHARD: We must take our pyjamas from the drawer marked pyjamas.

MRS OGMORE-PRITCHARD: (Coldly) And then you must take them off.

Dylan Thomas

***

Discussion

Dylan Thomas' writing is noted for its vividness. He rarely tells through statements when he can show through images...'An icicle forms in the cold air of the dining-vault'. What is suggested to you by the images below?

a) 'And before you let the sun in, mind it wipes its shoes.'
b) 'Mr Pugh reads, as he forks the shroud meat in...'
c) 'Clouds sag and pillow on Llareggub Hill.'

*

He makes full use of the sounds words make too, especially repeated sounds. When Mr. Ogmore and Mr. Pritchard 'reluctantly sigh and sidle', you can hear their rustling movements. What effect do repeated sounds have here?

a) "The sea lolls, laps and idles in.'
b) 'his needling stalactite hag and bednag of a pokerbacked nutcracker wife.'
c) 'in a hiss and prussic circle of cauldrons.'

*

How might it be possible for actors to suggest, through the way they repeat their instructions, different personalities for Mr. Ogmore and Mr. Pritchard? What sounds might be heard while Mr and Mrs Pugh are at table? In what tone should Mrs Pugh make her speech beginning, 'I saw you talking to a saint this morning...'? Which words should she emphasize? Where might it be possible to include music, and what kind?

*

Like the other two extracts in this section of the book, this one is from the script of a radio play. What differences does it make that such an excerpt is to be heard only, not seen and heard? To make full use of what's in the script, the producer would need to discuss its possibilities with his/her team:

The producer's assistant (to write directions/notes on the script)
eight actors and actresses
someone to decide on sound effects
and someone to choose appropriate music

The people responsible for sound effects and music will pass on their ideas to the producer's assistant who will note them on the script. The actors will be rehearsing together (paying attention to pace, to pauses and tones of voice), discussing with each other and the producer anything they don't understand. In overall charge, the producer will also be deciding, for example, how the recording should begin. In groups, and making use of this outline, use a cassette recorder to produce versions of this excerpt from 'Under Milk Wood'. Afterwards, compare notes on the differences you've noted in the recordings.

Taken Out

The play's characters are fictional but the events at its centre are real enough. In 1982, Argentinian armed forces invaded the Falkland Islands which had been governed from Britain. The Argentinian government had long laid claim to the islands. Its soldiers included men from Patagonia, an area settled by the Welsh during the last century. After fierce fighting, British troops reoccupied the Falklands — but not before, amongst other losses, the Sir Galahad had been hit and thirty-two Welsh Guardsmen on board killed. (The Argentinians meanwhile, when the General Belgrano was sunk with even greater loss of life, had their own cause for bitterness.) In these extracts, an English officer in the Welsh Guards, Peter Sommers, is remembering his horrific experience on the Sir Galahad. He finds it difficult to talk to his wife about it. But he still corresponds with Juan, an Argentinian whom he knew as a prisoner after the Falklands were retaken.

Characters:
PETER
JANE
JUAN
SERGEANT
OFFICER
SOLDIER 1
SOLDIER 2

SOLDIER 1: Captain Sommers! Help me, sir! Over here! This man's bleeding! His leg! His leg, sir!

PETER: He takes me to a man. I know him. He's lying on the deck screaming, leg ripped off in an explosion, pumping blood. The deck's hot, the blood hissing as it splatters. I didn't know what to do. I try picking him up, get him to a lifeboat — don't know how to.

SOLDIER 2: Leave! Leave! Leave! Leave me! Leave me! Captain, please!

PETER: Dragging him to the side.

SOLDIER 2: Take me out! Please! I don't want anymore.

PETER: Some nets have been thrown over. I lift him. What did I think I was doing? (Pause) I thought I could climb down, pass him down into the lifeboat. An officer is in it giving orders. He saw me.

OFFICER: Pull away! Pull away!

*

JANE: What's so difficult about actually talking to me?

(Long pause)

PETER: Nothing.

JANE: They did a great job on you, didn't they? Was this part of the training? It's a shame you left the Army, it's rather wasted on me. It's a shame they never trained you how to deal with it afterwards. (silence) Do you talk to Juan?

PETER: Not really, not in letters. We did though.

JANE: What's he like?

(Pause)

PETER: He's ... pretty normal sort of...

JANE: Was he like that when you met him?

PETER: He was in a bit of a state! All the prisoners were. They'd been on the islands for two and a half months. They stank. We let them shower every day. We fed them too. We looked after them.

JANE: I thought you would have hated them.

PETER: Some lads thought this was their chance, y'know, revenge. You can understand it. They'd been on *Sir Galahad*. They wanted something out of it.

JANE: What about the Argies?

PETER: All pretty terrified, I think.

JANE: Did you find Juan?

PETER: No, a sergeant told me about him.

SERGEANT: Sir. Argentine prisoner. He speaks English.

PETER: I had him brought up on deck. I wanted to find out how he saw it. If he hated me.

JANE: Why?

PETER: I suppose I was trying to find out why the pilot dropped those bombs.

SERGEANT: Prisoner attention! Prisoner for you, sir.

PETER: Hello.

(Pause. Juan looks at them.)

JUAN: Are you going to kill us?

PETER: What?

JUAN: Are you going to gas us?

PETER: Don't be ridiculous.

JUAN: Pardon?

PETER: No. We're not going to gas you.

(Pause)

JUAN: You take us to Argentina?

PETER: Yes.

PETER: (Out of scene) There was this awful pause, them waiting for me to speak. (In scene) I...do you realise...are...you...

JUAN: Ah! You have trouble with English. No problem, we speak Welsh.

PETER: What?

JUAN: Welsh. You Welsh Guards?

PETER: Yes.

JUAN: We speak Welsh. Fine!

PETER: No. No I don't speak Welsh actually.

JUAN: How come?

SERGEANT: The captain will ask the questions, boy.

PETER: Why do you ask?

JUAN: I speak Welsh more than English.

SERGEANT: You speak Welsh?

JUAN: Sure.

SERGEANT: Bloody hell! (In Welsh: Where are you from then?)

JUAN: (I was born in Patagonia. We play rugby there. Now we've moved. My father is a docker.)

PETER: What's he saying?

SERGEANT: Pardon me for one moment, sir. (In Welsh: How come you're fighting for them?)

JUAN: (I could ask the same of you.)

PETER: What's he saying, Sergeant?

SERGEANT: Nothing Sir. The lad speaks Welsh, sir. He's a Welshman, plays rugby, sir. His dad's a docker same as mine.

*

PETER: He shouldn't have said that. I wanted to come at it my own pace. Creep up on it. Waste. I always ask now. I asked your father, anyone who's seen action. I wait and drop the big one: 'Yes, but don't you feel an enormous sense of waste?'

Greg Cullen

***

Discussion

Why might the officer in the lifeboat have yelled 'Pull away!' (line 14) rather than staying to help those on board the ship, do you think?

*

'They did a great job on you, didn't they?' Jane asks Peter (line 18). What do you think she means?

*

Having read what he says earlier, what do you think Peter's feelings are as he speaks to Juan for the first time, and Juan asks 'Are you going to kill us?' (line 47) ?

*

Why does Juan assume that Peter's hesitation is because he has 'trouble with English' (line 58)?

*

'I could ask the same of you,' says Juan (line 77). What does he mean?

*

Do you agree with the sergeant that 'he's a Welshman' (line 80)?

*

What does Peter mean when he uses the word 'waste' (line 84)? And why did he want to 'come at it my own pace'?

*

On his return home to Patagonia, Juan tells his parents his version of the meeting with Peter and the Sergeant. Write out the dialgue, keeping in mind that Juan's father and mother would know little of war.

Suggestions

Oral

Having perfomed scripted pieces earlier in groups, try unscripted ones now, roughly sketching out the situation in discussion beforehand. Here are some possible starting points:

A family is looking forward to the arrival home of a daughter/son who has been abroad for a year or two and, unknown to them, got married. The announcement is made. The son's/daughter's partner is not, it soon appears, what the family might have hoped for.

Members of a local rock band are planning future gigs; one of them is about to break the news that he/she wants to leave the band.

Someone has disappeared, the friend of a group discussing the situation. What has happened to her/him? As various ideas are put forward, different responses to the friend emerge.

Writing

You could develop and polish a piece of dialogue you wrote or improvised earlier. Alternatively, choose a short story from the 'Relationships' section (or at least a part of it) and, bearing in mind the demands of radio, transform it into a play. Or write a new piece of dialogue, perhaps choosing one of these titles: I spy strangers; The discovery; Something is moving.

Portraits

a poetry workshop

Gossip, according to the poet W.H. Auden, is a kind of popular art: like writers, gossips are endlessly fascinated by people. Most of us spend quite a lot of time thinking and talking about others, trying to make sense of them. This section of the book focuses on poems about individual people, word portraits which try to catch a person's inner self through sharp glimpses rather than full-length studies.

Case History

There was a boy of twelve who'd never learned
To speak. Farm-bred, he had not understood
That he was more than livestock — turned
To dogs for company, came running for his food
With cats or chickens and woke with no surprise
At owls' homecoming or stars' breath on his face.
I saw him when they brought him in. His eyes
Were clear as sunlit water, held a space
We promptly crammed with language. Beyond reach
Soft wordless songs, the colours in wet stone
He loved; grass-smell; the old humanity of touch.
His brightness died and we began to realise
Speech wakes in us so confident, so soon,
What deeper dumbnesses might it disguise?

Christine Evans

Writing

After one class had talked about 'Case History', they wrote poems of their own about people, from memory, imagination, or based on photographs chosen from a collection. Here are two fragments:

> She passes.
> Hair streams behind like wisps of smoke.
> Walks like a grey mare.
>
> His chequered old worn-out slippers
> scratched across the pavement
> that seemed so long.
> Then the ambulance came that takes men away
> who wear pyjamas to go to town.

Before starting your own poem, see if this quiz for the imagination helps you start. Think of someone you could write about. Jot down your answers, where possible saying more than a few words.

1. If this person were a season, what season would he or she be?

2. And which colour?

3. In which detail of the face — nose, mouth, eyes — is this person's character best suggested?

4. What runs down the main street of this person's mind?

5. 'He is all pine and I am apple orchard,' said the poet Robert Frost of his darkly suspicious neighbour. What images best sum-up your relationship with this person?

Adding to your notes now (or scrapping them and going your own way), start on your poem.

*

The first draft of any piece of writing can usually be improved on. There will be too many words perhaps, or words that don't say enough. The class which produced the poems quoted earlier looked at copies of this early version of a poem by a fifteen-year-old:

Neighbour

He's sixty and kneels
in his home, the garden.
He ? the days of his life,
weeding his way through them.
Even at night the echo
of a lawn mower rings in his ears.
Cars pass all day but he doesn't hear.
His spade with an echo
scrapes, hitting the ground.
A stream of dreams flows
through the ? grass and shrubs,
cutting towards the rockery.

The lines were discussed. What should fill the gap in line three? 'He plants,' said someone. 'He grows,' said someone else. Most preferred 'grows', something more continuous. And what about the gap in the twelfth line? There were several suggestions: bright, wet, long. 'Why put anything there?'

Any other comments, suggestions? Someone pointed out that lines 5-8 seemed in the wrong order: the reference to day interrupts the lines about night and dreaming. Another voice didn't like line nine but couldn't say why. Because you don't need 'scrapes' *and* 'hitting'?

There were other points and questions. Why say how old he is? Because it's more realistic: the description seems more true of someone fairly old. Why are almost all the sentences two lines long? Sounds like a robot talking. Why repeat 'echo'. The following poem was the revised version most agreed with.

Neighbour

He's sixty and kneels
in his home, the garden.
He grows the days of his life,
weeding his way through.
Cars pass all day
and he doesn't hear
but even at night the echo
of a lawn mower rings in his ears.
His spade scrapes.
Stream of dreams flows
through the grass and shrubs,
cutting towards the rockery.

***

The following two poems by published poets are followed by their comments on them.

Rhys

Best of all I see him in the evening,
The stock of a shotgun cooling behind
A coat, woodpigeon's down plastered
Over his shirtfront. A guilty look,
But laughter under a shock of glossy curls:
Rhys, a squat Mediterranean type
Who kept his dirty tan all winter long.

We watched him over the kitchen table,
His son and I, as he broke down
A carburettor, the black grease oozing
From the opened valves, pieces of wrecked
Motorbike spread over the yard.
He talked of the job in the tinplate works
And the way the glowing metal sheets,

Incandescent as lava, came rolling
Towards him, the taste of his own sweat
In his mouth. That was the living
They gave him. Much better the one
He made himself, tuning the huge
Coughing Triumphs to full-throttled song,
Spinning them round in deafening

Rodeos over the mountainside,
Or setting out on evening expeditions,
Bringing us with him in a race downhill,
Glimpsing the moths he dashed from the grass,
Rising like sparks and vanishing,
Running headlong down to the invisible
Ffornwg, its high current moving east

And away, a crown of foam winking
Like beer-froth. And then he'd slip aside,
Deft hands and a murderous purpose
Opening the wire around private land
And I would wait, thinking of the pigeon
Plucked and headless, the rusted bones
Of metal that he wrenched from the machine.

Robert Minhinnick

Robert Minhinnick
talks about 'Rhys'

'Rhys' is one of a large number of poems that I wrote about the place where I was brought up — Pen-y-Fai, Mid-Glamorgan. In fact, thinking about it, my poetry could be said not really to have graduated far from that square mile of woods, fields, farms and industrial remnants. Today the area has suffered rather from 'gentrification', but is still identifiable.

Rhys was an outsider. Whether deliberately so, or because he was forced to be, is hard to say. He lived with his family 100 yards from me, and his son was my best friend. ('After a Friendship' in my book 'Native Ground' is an attempt to explain that relationship.) He stood out, I suppose. A bit of a rascal, unpredictable, unafraid, unconventional. He had a poacher's glamour. This was intensified by the feeling that other people in the village did not approve of him. Not that he worried.

I wrote the poem in Spring '81, and reading it again, I realize it is one I have put aside. Not forgotten about, but not returned to. Also it is not one that I have ever read at poetry readings. I don't know why. I remember writing it very quickly, and feeling surprised and pleased at the end when the images of the plucked bird and the motorbike seemed to come together. Perhaps I would change the shape of the poem now, and perhaps rejig the lines that start

> 'Or when he made...
>
> ...a head of foam
> Winking like beer froth'

There seems a great rush of writing there that might have been controlled better. But then, looking at the poem, I remember its spontaneity, and the excitement of writing it. (Why I should have written in Spring '81 about events at the beginning of the '60s, I can't think. Except that they were vivid and real.) And I suppose I am writing today about the same place, only relying less on memories than what is actually happening now.

Uncle Billy in the front room

Lemon- and biscuit-coloured light.
The oilcloth under the highframed bed
dusted clean, lightflooded
and me and my younger brother
shy children with the invalid.

We would like a bed pushed in the sun,
a frame like that to keep the blankets
off our legs.

He laughs and makes us exercise,
pedal air. Keep fit, he says.

But this is something absolute and good
and 'uncle' no relation, just his name.
The shrunken man, unshaven, spectacled, thin,
is misread as permanent.
Uncle Billy ambered in light and memory.

So fine to be tubercular like this:
a room with a bed,
a suntrapped, latticed bookcase.

Fixed in light on
a bookspine of a tale of castaways
a hero clambers an exotic hill.

Christopher Meredith

Christopher Meredith

talks about 'Uncle Billy'

This is the fourth in a set of six poems about a village called Troedrhiwgwair near Tredegar in south Wales. It draws on childhood memories of visits there in the late fifties and early sixties. I think it works best when you read the other poems around it. It's full of images of light and this contrasts with the previous poem, which starts and ends with images of darkness. In the previous poem, too, there's an image of live wasps trapped struggling in jam. I remember seeing them in a jar on the windowsill in the shadowy backyard of the house. The image is picked up in 'Uncle Billy' when I and my younger brother 'pedal air' and also later in the word 'ambered'. I thought of those insects that get stuck in resin and perfectly preserved for ever. This is picked up towards the end in 'suntrapped'. The poem ends with an image of climbing. I think the book was *The Swiss Family Robinson* and I, or my memory, cheated a bit, because the picture of the castaway climbing a lush hill was on the front of the book, not the spine. But I don't think that matters. There are images of climbing in some of the other poems and I hope a thoughtful reader would connect them. I've given enough away. My uncle's dead and most of the village has been demolished, but it gives me pleasure to think that a poem may have caught a little bit of it. I hope it's better than a lump of amber, though, and has a kind of life.

***

Writing

Having read these last two poems and comments, are there any improvements you could make in the poem you wrote earlier? Perhaps there are too many words at times, certain lines could be tightened. Do you have any flat statements which should be interesting images? And could your portrait be more fully developed, with additional detail? A poem, it's often been said, is never finished but abandoned...

*

Portraits needn't be serious, of course. Here are two which aren't, which in part use fantasy to light up reality.

Continent Isolated

There was a Fog in our pub the other night.
He trailed his native element with him. Fog
Came out of his ears; when he opened his mouth
What came up was pure Fogspeak. He discussed
At length and in detail his illnesses, and his wife's
Illnesses, and his wife's relatives' illnesses,
All caused, of course, by fog, and the fate of
His country, dear old Fogland. As he denounced
The politicians, fog oozed out of his boots. Too soft,
He reckoned, to Frogs and Wogs. We Fogs
Do all the slog, he said, not like them slobs,
All they can do is snog and flog grog, can't
Even build a decent bog, the Frog. As
For good old fogfood, nothing like it, bacon
And fog for breakfast, fog and chips, and
Don't forget, none of them foreigners have got
A Royal Foggily. As he went out
All the foghorns sounded for him on the other side.

Harri Webb

My Gran

My Gran feeds the cat
on bits of cheese,
on bits of chocolate biscuit
crumbled up;
the cat isn't very pleased.
She calls her 'Pussy Puss' —
sometimes she calls the cushion
by the same name.

My Gran burns kettles,
burns meals-on-wheels,
has been known to burn
a hole in her dress;
accuses the Home Help
of stealing her handkerchiefs.
Finds hankies, and washes them
dirtier than they were before.

My Gran falls through the floor
every morning, needs cups of tea
to bring her round to insanity,
needs glasses of sherry
to help her forget
that she can't remember.
Phones the butcher
to phone the doctor.

Lays tea at five
and supper at nine,
asks her dead husband
the time of year,
the day of time.
Blocks her bedroom door
with a bulky bureau
which screams every night
like a ghost.
My Gran likes only one
piece of toast
for tea and breakfast.

My Gran plays patience
and cheats,
drinks only one glass
of sherry a day,
and two bottles in half a week.
Threatens to have me turned out,
to call the police.

She's mad, I think,
or the clocks have stopped.

Mike Jenkins

Writing

Try writing your own comic poem with overtones of fantasy. If you like, write one about a hopeless zoo keeper being criticized by his boss. Everything has gone wrong for him. You could start with these lines then carry on rhyming:

When you came to work here, Mayles,
This was the largest zoo in Wales.

Or write a poem about someone who has grown increasingly like his/her pet — like the parrot owner with feathery hair who caws noisily, clawing money from his pocket.

*

One member of the class mentioned earlier decided to place himself in the mirror of his mind, and came up with this self-portrait:

I see

I see myself as a knife sometimes,
sharp, clean and confident,
ready to strike,
ready to pounce,
ready for the fight.

I see myself as a computer sometimes,
quiet, memorising and learning,
ready to work,
ready to try,
ready (almost) to do the exam.

Sometimes I see myself as a cloud,
dreamy, light and sleepy,
ready to fall,
ready to sway,
ready for the night of day.

Lawrence McLauchlan (15)

*

The poem is made up of three portraits really. How many people are you?

*

Here are two portraits with which to end. One of them is sharply realistic but the other makes use of fantasy to enter its subject's mind.

Elegy for Wiffin

You lived by us in Fothergill Street, but
my mother always kept me from playing with you.
You were sure to come to a bad end, she said,
with your name in The Pontypridd Observer.
For that, I wanted to be your butty, Wiffin,

especially when, on summer evenings,
the railway-siding's gorse was set alight
and the neighbours put the likely blame on you;
watching the fire-brigade from my window,
I took your part against their brazen tongues.

Why did you go and die like that?
Mitching from school, it was a wet Friday,
we balanced like two small Blondins
along the girders at Glyn-tâf weir — until you fell,
Wiffin, into the river and drowned.

What the police expected to discover
by pumping the industrial water away,
I was too brave to ask. Under the arc-lamps
the reeking mud yielded nothing but its own depths.
I could have told them you weren't there

for during the next few weeks, you and I
played together in all the prohibited places:
you showed me how to prise lead from factory roofs
and smash the sodium lights on Llantwit Road.
I felt your presence in my delinquent arm.

It wasn't until your withered body
fouled the cooling-tower's nets at Upper Boat,
two miles down the valley, I had to admit
that it was all over between us: from then on
I would have to watch my step, like a good boy.

Meic Stephens

The Hunchback in the Park

The hunchback in the park
A solitary mister
Propped between trees and water
From the opening of the garden lock
That lets the trees and water enter
Until the Sunday sombre bell at dark

Eating bread from a newspaper
Drinking water from the chained cup
That the children filled with gravel
In the fountain basin where I sailed my ship
Slept at night in a dog kennel
But nobody chained him up.

Like the park birds he came early
Like the water he sat down
And Mister they called Hey mister
The truant boys from the town
Running when he had heard them clearly
On out of sound.

Past lake and rockery
Laughing when he shook his paper
Hunchbacked in mockery
Through the loud zoo of the willow groves
Dodging the park keeper
With his stick that picked up leaves.

And the old dog sleeper
Alone between nurses and swans
While the boys among willows
Made the tigers jump out of their eyes
To roar on the rockery stones
And the groves were blue with sailors

Made all day until bell time
A woman figure without fault
Straight as a young elm
Straight and tall from his crooked bones
That she might stand in the night
After the locks and chains

All night in the unmade park
After the railings and the shrubberies
The birds the grass the trees the lake
And the wild boys innocent as strawberries
Had followed the hunchback
To his kennel in the dark.

Dylan Thomas

***

Discussion

Some people like mainly poetry that's direct and clear like 'Elegy for Wiffin'. Others prefer a more richly demanding poetry. How demanding do you find 'The Hunchback in the Park' ?

*

The poem asks you to make a mental leap into the hunchback's mind. He's nameless, a mere 'mister' seen by others as hardly more that a thing 'propped' against the park. Why 'Sunday sombre'?

*

The boys 'made tigers jump out of their eyes' perhaps because they were playing a jungle game. They're together, completely involved. In contrast, what do bread, water and the chained cup in the second stanza suggest about the hunchback's life?

*

Why does he keep returning to the park? Why should he have needed to imagine 'a woman figure without fault? 'Why can't the poem be simpler?' an impatient reader might ask. To which the poet might answer: 'Are people simple? Is life?'

The Earth

Reportage

In its early days, it was thought that radio might damage the popularity of newspapers, then later that television would do so. But, despite the obvious appeal of these media, newspaper circulations have continued to rise. Good newspapers can explain things in a more organised, leisurely way. What the journalist writes, uncluttered by sounds and moving pictures, might well remain longer than rapid television reports in the reader's mind. The fact that the reader has chosen to focus on a particular news item helps too. Whether or not it's worth reading will depend on the quality of the journalism. In quality journalism, the playwright Alan Bennet has said, 'Accuracy isn't a virtue, it is a duty'. Obviously the journalist has a duty to research a story thoroughly, to record the facts. Also involved though is the appropriate use of those facts; even common truths can be distorted. And, thirdly, the facts need to be conveyed in a clear, well-organised way. Writing something that's absolutely accurate and clear isn't always easy. What unintended meanings can you find in these headlines from actual newpapers?

Juvenile court to try shooting defendant

Shouting Match Ends Teacher's Hearing

Firebombing Jury Takes Weekend Off

Man Robs, Then Kills Himself

Lucky Man Sees Pals Die

The pages that follow contain examples of Green journalism, newspaper and magazine articles related to the environment.

Acid Rain in Snowdonia

Acid deposition in Europe (created by the combustion of fossil-fuels and by motor engines) is now widely regarded as a disastrous phenomenon of environmental destruction. However, despite much publicity and valuable research work in Wales by bodies such as the Welsh Water Authority, the Institute of Terrestrial Ecology and Friends of The Earth, there is a marked reluctance by government and the Forestry Commission to admit that our own environment is suffering from the effects of acid rain, mist and snow.

This curious inertia has been highlighted by the response to the 'Acid Rain in Snowdonia' document, released late last year by the Snowdonia National Park Authority. This short paper makes alarming reading for anyone at all concerned with the health of this magnificent part of our natural environment. It describes how both freshwater and vegetation in Snowdonia are now exhibiting symptoms of acid damage.

For example, 'acidification in Llyn Conwy, once regarded as one of the best trout fishing lakes in Snowdonia, has virtually destroyed the fish population'. Llyn Cwm Mynach, Llyn Dulyn, Llyn Eiddaw Bach, Llyn Llagai and Llyn y Bi are also acidified. Llyn Gamallt is so seriously polluted that when attempts were made to restock the lake with trout, the fish died of 'acid stress' within two days.

Trees in the National Park, especially beech, ash, oak, yew and Scots pine, are also in decline, exhibiting reduced crown density, early or unnatural yellowing, needle-loss, and less resistance to fungi, pests and insect-damage. (In this way, the effects of acid deposition on trees can be likened to those of AIDS on mankind. The pollution might not kill the tree outright, but due to its fundamentally weakening influence, it encourages fatal assaults from other sources that might well have been withstood by a healthy specimen.)

Snowdonia is especially vulnerable to acid deposition because of the naturally acidic nature of its geology and the poor buffering capacity of its thin soils. North Wales rain, ironically, is amongst the least-polluted in Europe, but because there is proportionally more of it, and the area has little chalk and limestone to neutralize the acid, the problem becomes more intense than in say the south-east of England.

It is apparent that the scale of this pollution problem has taken the Welsh Office by surprise. Despite the Llyn Brianne research project carried out by the Welsh Water Authority in mid Wales, and the research of the

Institute of Terrestrial Ecology in the Beddgelert Forest, there is no specific Welsh Office initiative aimed at discovering just what acid deposition is doing to its national parks.

However, there are reasons for this lack of activity by the Welsh Office. Incredibly, in the twelve months before June 21 this year, the Secretary of State for Wales had received only two representations on the threats posed by air pollution to Snowdonia. (Energy Minister Cecil Parkinson was smugly able to inform members of Friends of The Earth and Greenpeace this year that the lack of letters to MPs on the subject of acid rain proved the lack of public concern.)

Moreover, the government's own (extremely belated and reluctant) steps to counter air pollution mean that sulphur emissions from fossil-fuel burning power-stations will be cut by only sixty per cent of 1980 figures by the year 2003.

Output of nitrogen oxide, the other major constituent of acid rain, will be diminished by thirty per cent by 1998. There are also plans to introduce new vehicle exhaust emission standards ('as soon as practicable'). Such actions, despite their cost, are seen by many conservation bodies as too little and too late. Indeed after years of the UK being described as the 'dirty man of Europe', and being universally held responsible for the 'export' of the pollution that has so devastated Scandinavian lakes, the measures can be seen to be the very minimum that the government could get away with. (It is generally agreed that sulphur and nitrogen emissions should be cut by at least ninty per cent to prevent further large-scale acidification of north and central Europe.)

This threat to Snowdonia — for good or ill, one of the most popular parts of Wales with tourists — comes when the market research of the Wales Tourist Board shows that it is quality of the Welsh environment that has the highest priority with visitors. Whether the WTB can find within itself the courage or the capability to lobby for more sensitive treatment of environmental issues is difficult to say. Apologists (or cynics) might state that that is not the nature of the beast. However, the Wales Tourist Board is obviously placed in a moral dilemma here. It certainly cannot continue blithely attempting to attract a greater stream of visitors to Snowdonia without taking a definite interest in the future health of the National Park. As the stickers say, acid rains on us all, and that includes the chief executives of organizations who believe that 'pollution' and 'the environment' are outside their remit.

Another major concern of the National Park Authority is that Forestry Commission plantations of conifers are adding to the acid build-up. The fine shallow root systems of these trees increase land drainage to such an extent that rain passes too quickly through the soil for its acidic charge to be neutralized. Moreover, acid rain itself washes aluminium salts out of the earth and into lakes and reservoirs. There is now a good deal of suspicion (if not hard evidence) that a concentration of aluminium in the human brain is responsible for premature senility (Alzheimer's Disease).

Thus the pollution threatens the direct physical health of people as well as that of trees and lakes. It has been calculated that nearly 1500 properties in Meirionnydd alone have their own private water supplies. There is no control over the quality of these waters, and it is entirely up to the consumers whether they wish to test either the acid or aluminium content of their supplies. One such test in 1987 revealed a 100-fold increase in acidity on a private supply since 1980. Another survey showed that a particular stream had three times the aluminium content considered a health maximum by the Welsh Water Authority.

Despite the lackadaisical approach of the Government to such matters (Mrs Thatcher was quoted at the time of the Falklands War as saying that it was exciting to be dealing with a *real* crisis after years of humdrum issues such as the 'environment'), there are initiatives planned regarding the effect of air pollution on Snowdonia. And in its own way, the 'Acid Rain in Snowdonia' paper is a watershed. It is the first such document to manifest concern at the impact of air pollution on a National Park, and is therefore to be widely welcomed, not least by the Welsh Office, as a particularly vivid depiction of what acid deposition is now doing to Wales.

Robert Minhinnick (1988)

***

Discussion

Bearing in mind the points made earlier, consider the extent to which this article can be called 'accurate'. It contains a lot of factual detail, for example, to support and illustrate its argument. Which single piece of evidence did you find the most interesting or significant?

*

The writer gives his sources too: the document released by the Snowdonia National Park Authority, the research done by the Institute of Terrestrial Ecology...Where does the reporter not give his source? And is a source necessary for each fact?

*

As regards the appropriateness of his use of facts, the reporter doesn't select only those which suit his argument. He admits that the rain in North Wales is 'among the least-polluted in Europe', that the Secretary of State for Wales had received only two concerned enquiries about air pollution in Snowdonia, that the government is taking some action. Do such admissions seem to you to make his argument more persuasive or less?

*

How organised and clear is the argument? Notice how the opening paragraphs progress from the general (acid deposits in Europe) to the particular (the problem in Snowdonia) to the more specific (its effects on lakes, trees, soil then people). Is that the best way? How does the Wales Tourist Board fit into the argument?

*

Do you find the writer's language clear? (Is it the reader's responsibility to find out the meanings of words which he or she may not understand?) For what kind of audience was the article written, do you think?

*

Obviously the writer's aim here was to persuade as well as inform. Is it only the government of whom he is critical?

*

'Incredibly...smugly...' Find three other words or phrases which indicate that he is expressing opinions, keen to persuade the reader.

Radioactive coast count is 100 times Chernobyl

MIKE SETTLE

TWO AREAS of the North Wales coastline are contaminated with radioactivity 100 time greater than those found near Chernobyl, environmentalists claimed last night.

Lavan Sands, near the Menai Straits, and the Dee Estuary in Clwyd, have alarmingly high levels of the radioactive plutonium and americium.

And the environmental pressure group Greenpeace claims the levels are much higher than those found thirty miles north of the Chernobyl reactor in 1986 after the worst nuclear accident the world has ever seen.

The claims are based on figures from an official report commissioned by the Government's own Inspectorate of Pollution.

Greenpeace says that discharges of radioactive effluent from the Sellafield reprocessing plant in Cumbria are responsible. The new claims will rekindle fears among locals, particularly in the Llanfairfechan area, near the Lavan Sands, who have been told by scientists in previous surveys that radioactivity levels were ten times higher than normal.

Caernarfon MP Dafydd Wigley commented 'It's a matter of very grave concern that dictates urgent scrutiny.

I have had indirect reports of this. There have been allegations of severe dumping of radioactivity in the Conwy Bay area supposed partly to be from Sellafield.

Scientists in Bangor have been working on this and although they said they found higher levels were not alarmed at this time.

But this new information is more recent and more worrying.'

A spokesman for Greenpeace commented, 'A study into radioactive contamination of Wales commissioned by HM Inspectorate of Pollution found that the Lavan Sands to the northeast of the Menai Straits and the estuary of the River Dee were nearly 100 times more contaminated with plutonium than an area 30 miles north of Chernobyl in 1986.'

The source of the study is given as *Artificial Radioactivity on the Coasts of Wales* by Garland Cambray Burton and McKay, Harwell Laboratory, 1990.

So far, of all the plutonium discharged into the Irish Sea, only one per cent has returned to land with eighty-five per cent remaining in coastal sediments of the Irish Sea, claims Greenpeace.

'With such a large proportion of the plutonium still in coastal sediments, the effects of local storms and flooding could bring more of Sellafield's radioactive pollution ashore,' said the spokesman.

He refers to research conducted after the Towyn floods which suggested there could be a radiological hazard.

This, however, has been hotly denied by several scientists, including Government officers, who have carried out several post-flood analyses.

Sampling equipment set up at Prestatyn and Dyserth in Clwyd detected plutonium and americium in the air and samples of rainfall taken at both places as well as Penmaenmawr and Porth Dinllaen.

The spokesman added, 'British Nuclear Fuels, who own and operate Sellafield, still discharge two million gallons of radioactive waste into the Irish Sea every day.'

***

Discussion

The first paragraph of a lead story, since it sums-up the most striking information, is often written in bold print. And it can reveal how accurate (or otherwise) the headline is. How important do you find the differences in the article on radioactivity between what is said in the headline and in the first paragraph?

*

In the first five paragraphs, the words 'claimed' and 'claims' are used four times. Why? Would 'said' or 'states' have been appropriate?

*

Why was the MP's comment included (paragraph six), do you think?

*

How clear do you find the article? Why is it the coast, not inland areas, that is vulnerable to the pollution described here? How could the pollution be reduced?

*

In terms of their information, what broad similarities have you noticed between the two reports you have read so far?

*

As in the following examples from the same editions of *Wales on Sunday*, the theme of a news report is often taken up in a regular column expressing a senior journalist's opinions. Read the two articles carefully and consider in what respects their styles differ.

Artist's impression of radar base

Plaid Cymru leaflet against the radar base

TOWERING £1BN BLOT ON LANDSCAPE

This is how one of Wales's most scenic areas will look if the Ministry of Defence has its way.

Our artist's impression of the massive £1bn military radar base planned for Pembrokeshire shows just how much of an impact it will have on the tranquil setting.

Protesters bitterly opposed to the joint US-UK project say the installation will devastate the local environment and cripple the tourist industry, which is the lifeblood of the area's economy.

Bulldozers will move in to start construction work next year unless the action group Pembrokeshire Against the Radar Campaign (PARC) wins its campaign.

The base will be built on a disused World War II airfield just outside the historic cathedral city of St David's.

The site will be around 85 acres, including a safety exclusion zone around the installation. In this area there will also be a single-storey temporary building and about 15 equipment containers.

The transmitter will consist of 35 aerials, each a metal lattice with masts and a wire running from the top to a smaller pole stationed in front of it. Copper aerial elements will be strung vertically from the wire.

Sixteen of these aerials will be 135 feet tall, the rest smaller.

The huge scale of the radar has infuriated local residents.

'People should appreciate the truly monstrous scale of the visual intrusion which would be inflicted on the flat-topped St Davids Peninsula' said Jim McBrearty, who has launched a one-man campaign against the development.

'If this huge eyesore were built, it would change the shape of the whole landscape.' PARC is equally outspoken about the impact the base will have on the environment.

Group treasurer Harry Poore said: 'It will obviously be a monstrous thing. There's an awful lot of concern about the effect it will have on the local economy.

Tourism is a crucial source of income in this area and we fear this will stop people coming.

Anyone can see it is going to be an ugly blot on the landscape.'

Wales on Sunday Reporter

***

JOHN OSMOND

WHERE SKYLARK AND JET FLY

When I wandered into a grocery store in the tiny village of Marloes on the Dale peninsula in Pembrokeshire one day last week, my eye was immediately caught by a pile of leaflets on the counter.

To each was stapled a rough sheet of paper with a hand-written note from John Barrett, a naturalist who lives nearby, and who is renowned throughout Wales as a writer on the flora and fauna of the county.

'Please read slowly and act quickly — John Barrett,' was the message.

Attached was a leaflet from PARC — the Pembrokeshire Against Radar Campaign — with a printed postcard addressed to the the Secretary of State for Defence, waiting to be signed, stamped and sent off to Whitehall.

The leaflet has a graphic drawing, showing radar pylons dwarfing St David's Cathedral.

It repeats what by now must be familiar arguments to those who have followed this saga, first revealed by *Wales on Sunday* in March.

The Ministry of Defence, in association with the American Department of Defense, plans to build 35, 125-foot-high 'over -the-horizon-radar' aerials on a disused airfield near St David's — metal lattice masts with copper aerial elements vertically strung from a wire which will run from the top of each aerial to a pole in front.

If they go ahead with the plan they will be like a giant electric fence, since they would give you a shock and severe burns if you touched them — hence the 85-hectare exclusion zone that is planned around the masts.

Controversially, it is claimed that they will emit radioactive waves harmful to humans and bird life, claims denied by the Ministry of Defence.

More potently for those who are campaigning against them, the aerials would be a symbol of Cold War aggression in an area famed for its mystical and peaceful associations, and in an era when the Cold War is deemed to be receding into history.

John Barrett's leaflet adds that the £1bn installation will bring no more than 19 jobs — information gleaned from a reply to a Parliamentary question — and will be a threat to the tourist economy of the area.

All this I took in, slowly, as John Barrett enjoined. Then my hand hovered over the postcard I was being asked to send off to Tom King at the Ministry of Defence.

'What possible effect could it have?' I asked myself, doubtless in that instant registering the reply to a Parliamentary questions — and will be a threat to the tourist economy of the area.

All this I took in, slowly, as John Barrett enjoined. Then my hand hovered over the postcard I was being asked to send off to Tom King at the Ministry of Defence.

'What possible effect could it have?' I asked myself, doubtless in that instant registering the powerlessness felt by most people when confronted with some distant, though horrendous, 'requirement of national security.'

Sending postcards, signing petitions, attending meetings, going on marches...what impact can they have in our comfortable society on powerful people and institutions for whom Pembrokeshire is merely an outline on the edge of a map?

As if to emphasise the thought, at that moment another low-flying training jet from the Brawdy air base knifed its noisy way across the sky.

With that I stuffed the leaflet, and John Barrett's message into the pocket of my jacket and trudged on along Pembrokeshire's coastal path, to the accompaniment of a skylark reasserting its insistent cry in the wake of the harsh reverberating throatiness of the low-flying military jet.

Yet I was unable to forget those radar masts for long. Everywhere I went in Pembrokeshire last week I was confronted with PARC posters and petitions — in shops, on lampposts and stuck on the door windows of almost every pub.

No doubt the powers that be will ignore the opposition. Somewhere has to have these masts, they will argue, and wherever they go they will provoke protest. Apparently, 166 possible sites throughout Europe have been examined.

It may be, however, that in choosing St David's the powers that be — in this case the Government — have overlooked a very real sanction local protesters will have to hand before too long.

This will come at the next election, when the local Tory MP, Nicholas Bennett, who has been equivocating on the radar base, could well become its first casualty.

Wales on Sunday
(10 June 1990)

***

Discussion

Discuss the following questions in small groups. Someone in each group should make notes in order to report the group's opinions to the class later.

*

What difference does the use of the first person ('When I wandered...') make to the voice you hear in the second article?

*

The writer of the second piece mentions the powerlessness felt by most individuals when faced by distant, massive authority. 'What impact can this have?' Which details in the second paragraph suggest that this is an unequal struggle? Does the first article contain similar details?

*

What differences do you note in the language contained in these pairs of extracts from the two articles?

a) 'The site will be around 85 acres, including a safety exclusion zone around the installation.'

'They will be like a giant electric fence, since they would give you a shock and severe burns if you touched them — hence the 85 acre exclusion zone that is planned around the masts.'

b) 'Protestors bitterly opposed to the joint US-UK project say the installation will devastate the local environment.'

'I...trudged on along Pembrokeshire's coastal path, to the accompaniment of a skylark reasserting its insistent cry in the wake of the harsh reverberating throatiness of the low-flying military jet.'

*

What wider issues is the columnist able to consider, for which the reporter has no space?

*

Which did you find the more persuasive piece? Why? Is there need for both kinds of journalism?

***

In 1990, J.A.A. Jones of the Institute of Earth Studies at Aberystwyth published in the magazine *Planet* an article entitled 'Greenhouse Wales'. It described the possible effects of global warming. The release of artificial gases into the atmosphere could be causing a rise in temperature which might possibly begin melting the West Antarctic Ice Sheet. The article included the map of Wales overleaf. It illustrates possible coastal flooding, changes in climate, coastal erosion, and the consequences for agriculture. Obviously it's bad news — but 'an enhanced Greenhouse Effect is clearly not all doom and gloom'. Write two newspaper reports, for *The Sun* and *The Guardian*, including headlines. Describe the processes indicated on the map and suggest their possible consequences. (The '7 metre Blue Belt' refers to land which would be flooded if the sea level rose by seven metres.)

GREENHOUSE WALES

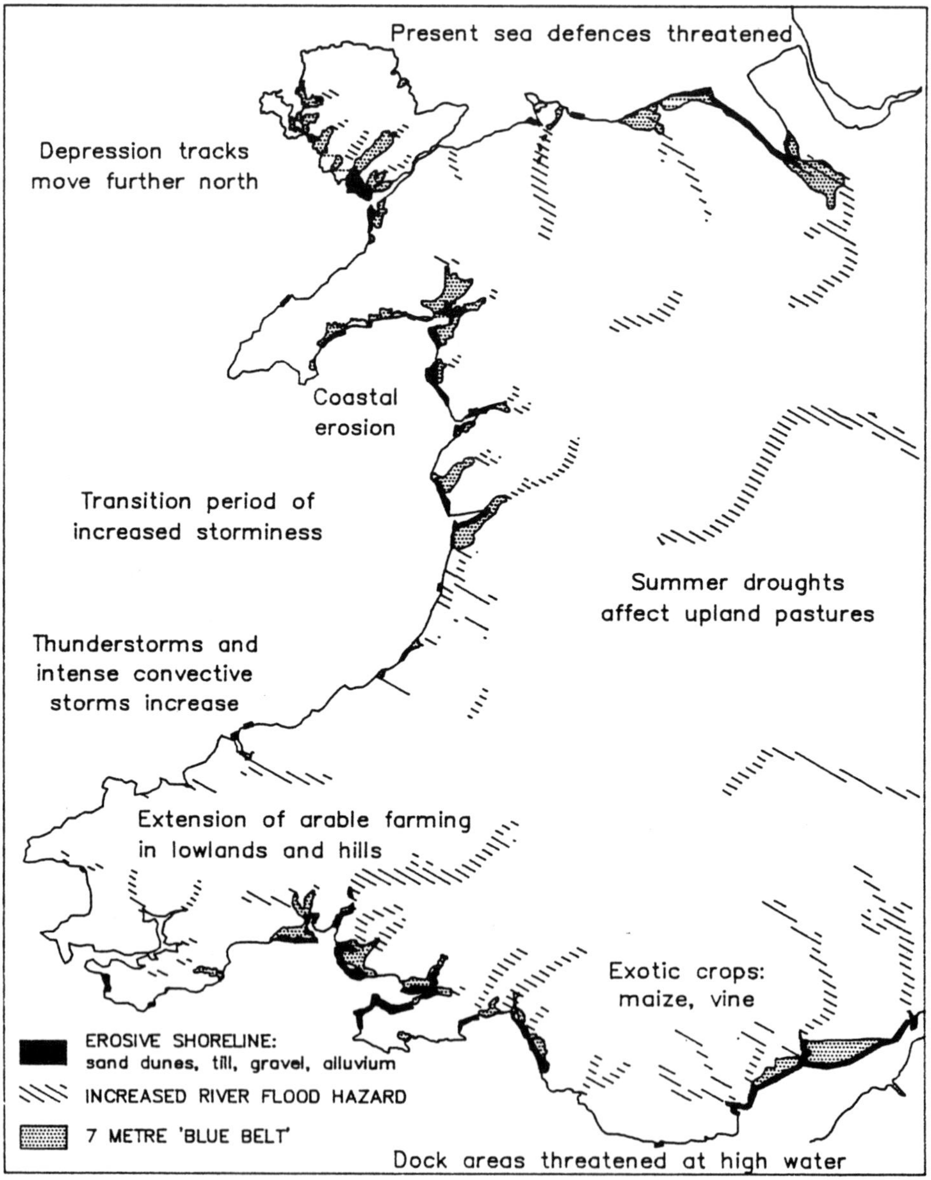

Suggestions

Oral

'There is little threat to our environment in this area': a class debate. There could be two speakers on each side, a chairperson, and contributions from the audience could follow those of the main speakers.

Hold a public enquiry arising from one of the issues raised in this section. Groups of pupils could represent the particular concerns of, for example, residents, naturalists, conservationists, parents, and a panel of experts or officials could respond to their questions and statements.

Writing

A newspaper is running a campaign with the slogan 'Cleaner World' in which readers are invited to write about any environmental issue which concerns them. Write a letter to the editor. (If possible, find some hard facts to support your case.)

'Disaster.' Write an imaginative piece (diary entries possibly) from the point of view of someone who has experienced a sudden flood, illustrated as a possibility earlier on the map of Wales.

Prepare a Green questionnaire for fourth and fifth-year students, testing attitudes to food, water and energy. Having completed this and analysed your returns, present your conclusions as a newspaper report.

*(Editor's note: The radar base plans have been abandoned)

Acknowledgements

We would like to thank the following authors, owners of copyright, publishers, literary agents and executors for permission to reprint the poems, plays and extracts of prose printed in this anthology.

Dannie Abse and Sheil Land Associates for *Ash on a Young Man's Sleeve* (Penguin, 1986).

Glenda Beagan for 'The Saddist' which first appeared in *Planet* (69, 1988) and 'Pink Summer Blues' — both included in her book of short stories, *The Medlar Tree* (Seren, 1992).

Estate of Euros Bowen for 'Bits and Pieces' from *Cerddi Rhydd* (Gwasg y Brython, Llandysul, 1961).

Duncan Bush for 'The Sea, The Sea' (*Poetry Wales*, Vol. 21.1), and *Poetry Wales: 25 Years* (Seren 1991).

Dorothy Chamberlain for the extract (and the small drawing) from Brenda Chamberlain's *Tide-race* (Hodder & Stoughton 1962), reprinted by Seren Books in 1987.

The estate of Bruce Chatwin for the extract from *On The Black Hill* (Cape, 1983).

Gillian Clarke for 'Foghorns' from *Selected Poems* (Carcanet, 1985).

Joseph Clancy for his translations of 'Horses' by Gwyn Thomas. His source is *Gwyn Thomas: Living a Life: Selected Poems 1962-82* (Bridges Books, Amsterdam, 1982). Also from *Twentieth Century Welsh Poems* (Gomer, 1982), and for 'Bits and Pieces' by Euros Bowen (see above).

Tony Connor for 'Above Penmaenmawr' from *Kon in Springtime* (Oxford University Press, 1968).

Greg Cullen for the extract from his play *Taken Out* (BBC Radio, Cardiff).

Tony Curtis for 'Pwllcrochan' from *Selected Poems* (Poetry Wales Press, 1986).

Lewis Davies for the estate of Rhys Davies for the extract from *Print of a Hare's Foot* (Heinemann, 1969).

The estate of Idris Davies for 'O What Can You Give Me? *Gwalia Deserta* (Dent, 1938).

John Davies for 'Things to do when the town's closed' from *Flight Patterns* (Seren, 1990).

Christine Evans for 'Case History' from *Poetry Wales* (Vol. 25.2, 1989) and to be included in her forthcoming collection *Island of Dark Horses*, and 'Exchange' and 'Summer in the Village' — both from *Looking Inland*, (Poetry Wales Press, 1983).

Jean Earle for 'In The Night' from *The Intent Look* (Gomer, 1984).

Cassandra Davies for the estate of Margiad Evans for the extract from her *Autobiography* , first published by Arthur Bashes in 1943. Also by Calder & Boyars in 1974.

Peter Finch for 'The Computer's First Proverbs' from his *Selected Poems* (Seren, 1987).

Emyr Humphreys for 'Pastoral' from *Ancestor Worship* (Gee, 1970).

John L. Hughes for the extract from *Before the Crying Ends*, (Bodley Head, 1977).

David Hughes for 'Swanzee Boy See?' from *Planet* (56, 1986).

Wil Ifan for 'The River and the Road' from *Wales Today* edited by D.Dale-Jones (Gomer, 1976).

Mike Jenkins for 'I' from *Empire of Smoke* (Poetry Wales Press, 1983) and 'My Gran' from *Common Land* (Poetry Wales Press, 1981).

Nigel Jenkins for 'Pig Killing Day' which first appeared in *The Green Horse* edited by Stephens and Finch (Christopher Davies, 1978) and subsequently in *Acts of Union: Selected Poems* (Gomer, 1990).

J. A. A. Jones for the map of Greenhouse Wales from *Planet* (82, 1990).

Alan Llwyd for 'Geese/Gwyddau' first published in *Poetry Wales* (Winter 1981) and reprinted with permission of Christopher Davies.

Lawrence McLauchlan for his previously unpublished poem 'I See'.

Christopher Meredith for 'Uncle Billy in the front room' from *Snaring Heaven* (Seren, 1990) and for his commentary on the poem.

Robert Minhinnick for 'Driving in Fog' and 'Rhys' — both from *Life Sentences* (Poetry Wales Press, 1983), for his commentary on 'Rhys', and for 'Acid Rain in Snowdonia' which first appeared in *Planet* (71, 1988).

Leslie Norris for his story 'A Moonlight Gallop' from *Sliding* (Dent, 1971), and his poems 'Dog' and 'Barn Owl' — both from his *Selected Poems* (Seren, 1986).

John Osmond for his article 'Where Skylark and Jet Fly' from *Wales on Sunday* (July 17, 1990).

Gwyn Parry for 'Porpoise' from *The Hurricane* (Poetry Wales Press, 1987).

Mike Settle for his article 'Radioactive Coast' from *Wales on Sunday* (July 17, 1990).

Janice Short for the extract 'Walking the Plank' from *On My Life*, edited by Verrill-Rhys (Honno, 1989).

Meic Stephens for 'Elegy for Wiffin' which first appeared in *Poetry Wales* and subsequently in *The Green Horse*, edited by Stephens and Finch (Christopher Davies, 1978).

David Higham Associates and the Dylan Thomas estate for the extracts from: 'Quite Early One Morning' (A Child's Christmas in Wales); 'Patricia, Edith and Arnold' from *Portrait of the Artist as a Young Dog* (Dent); *Under Milk Wood* (Dent); and 'The Hunchback in the Park' from *Collected Poems* (Dent).

Gwyn Thomas for 'Horses' as translated by Joseph Clancy in *Twentieth-Century Welsh Poems* (Gomer,1982).

R.S. Thomas for 'Welsh History' from *Song at the Year's Turning* (Hart-Davis, 1963) and 'The Chapel' from *Laboratories of the Spirit* (Macmillan, 1975).

Jean Henderson for the estate of John Tripp for 'Weasels' from *Dragon's Hoard* (Gomer, 1976).

Gwen Watkins for the estate of Vernon Watkins for 'The Collier', first published in *The Ballad of the Mari Lwyd* (Faber & Faber, 1941).

Charles Way for the extract from his play *Funny Boys,* first produced by Gwent Theatre and subsequently broadcast by BBC Radio Wales, Cardiff, and BBC Radio 4, London, on 'Saturday Night Theatre'.

Harri Webb for 'Synopsis of the Great Welsh Novel' from *The Green Desert* (Gomer, 1969) and 'Continent Isolated' from *A Crown for Branwen* (Gomer, 1974).

The estate of Emlyn Williams for the extract from *George* (Hamish Hamilton, 1988).

Frances Williams for 'The Foghorn' from *Flotsam* (Poetry Wales Press, 1987).

Sir Ifor Williams for 'I Am Taliesin' (Anon.) from *Lectures on Early Welsh Poetry* (Dublin, 1944). It is here reprinted from his *The Poems of Taliesin,* English version by J.E. Caerwyn Williams (Dublin, 1968).

Wales on Sunday for the article 'Towering £1Bn Blot' from July 17, 1990.

Artists

Chris Bayley for his wood engravings: view to accompany 'Walking the Plank' (p. 31), view to accompany foghorn poems (p. 44), lantern to accompany 'A Moonlight Gallop' (p. 75), owl to accompany 'Barn Owl' (p. 119).

Dorothy Chamberlain for the estate of Brenda Chamberlain for her ink drawings from *Tide-Race* (pp. 28).

Stephen Dalton for his photograph of a greenshank (p. 167), originally published in *Secret Lives: 25 Years of Nature Photography* (Century Hutchinson, 1988).

Martin Dunkerton for his photograph 'Satellites and Sunglasses, Merthyr Vale, 1990', originally published in 'Is it Still Raining in Aberfan?' (Logaston Press) 1991 (p.11).

Andrew Erskine for his cartoons to accompany 'Synopsis of the Great Welsh Novel' (p. 49), and 'My Gran' (p. 161).

Mick Felton for his portrait photograph of Robert Minhinnick (p. 156).

J.A. A. Jones for his map of 'Greenhouse Wales' (p. 182) originally published in *Planet* 82, 1988.

Rhianedd Thomas for her ink drawings to accompany 'A Child's Christmas in Wales' (p. 23), 'Patricia, Edith, and Arnold' (p. 84), and 'Under Milk Wood' (p. 141).

Margaret Salisbury for her photographs: 'The Triangle' (p.19), 'Path in the Valley' (p. 37), 'Birdman' (p. 64), Boy, Girl and Dog (p. 71), 'The Wall' (p. 94), 'Sheepdog' (p. 105), 'Fresh Pork' (p. 115), 'Beside the Sea' (p. 131), 'Dai Dant' (p.163).

Ernest Zobole for his cover painting 'Looking Out, 1986'.

Author Index